Graphic Des
Desktop Dummies

Marvin Jacobs
President
Ameritype & Art Inc.
Cleveland, Ohio

*The Best is the Enemy
of the Good.*

— Voltaire

Published by
Ameritype & Art Inc.
Cleveland

AMERITYPE
724 KEITH BUILDING
1621 EUCLID AVENUE
CLEVELAND, OH 44115
216-696-4545

ISBN 0-9629700-1-8

Library of Congress Catalog Card Number: 92-75564

Requests for permission to make copies of any part of the work should be mailed
to: Permissions, Ameritype & Art, 724 Keith Building, 1621 Euclid Avenue, Cleveland,
Ohio 44115, 216-696-4545.

Printed in the United States of America

PREFACE

In the early days of printing, the printer was the graphic designer and the printer. As demands for printed documents increased and printing became more mechanized, a division of skills developed between the printer and the designer. Graphic designing developed into a separate occupation.

The objective of the designer was to design the document to clearly and effectively communicate information. That was the objective then and it is still the objective now.

Until the relatively recent use of computers and desktop publishing to create graphic designs, designers did their work with pens and markers on paper. Designs for advertisements, magazines, books and other documents were usually created by trained graphic designers.

Now, with easy access to personal computers and graphics software, an increasing number of ineffectual designs are being created by untrained designers. They have marvelous design tools but they have not had graphic design training. Buying a Stradivarious does not automatically make one a concert violinist.

To compound the problem, the untrained computer designer is also now the untrained typesetter. Previously the designer drew the design and gave it to the typesetter who created the camera-ready art for the printer. Now the untrained designer is also the untrained typesetter because desktop publishing allows the design and the typesetting to be done simultaneously.

This technologically-created change in the design work flow has the advantage of convenience and also potential savings in time and money but the burden is on the computer typist who has to learn to operate the computer and to learn software programs, graphic design and typesetting.

Computer and software training is available from other sources. The objective of this book is to help the computer typist with graphic design and typesetting training.

Computers and software programs are only tools. Good graphic design and good taste are not default settings. Computers and software programs change constantly but graphic design principles stay the same. Of course there are time periods in which trends and fads affect design but graphic design is solidly based on timeless and traditional graphic principles.

ACKNOWLEDGMENTS

I am indebted to Sharon Jacobs for the splendid typesetting and computer-aided illustrations and for her advice and support.

I am also indebted to Ron Strzelecki for the professional graphic camera prints for illustrations and for the impeccable paste-up job.

Contents

GRAPHIC DESIGN BASICS

GRAPHIC DESIGN FOR SPECIFIC APPLICATIONS

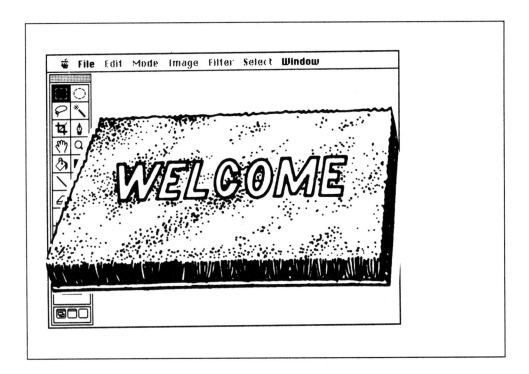

Chapter One
Introduction to Graphic Design

*If you want your dreams
to come true, don't sleep.*

— *Yiddish Proverb*

1 Introduction to Graphic Design

A graphic design drawn by hand.

The graphic designer doesn't need to be an artist.

WHAT IS GRAPHIC DESIGN?

Graphic design is the conversion of ideas into an organized visual layout. The design is usually drawn by hand or created with a computer using a desktop or other software program. The resulting visual layout is usually used to (1) make a presentation for approval and then (2) serve as a guide or camera copy for the production of a printed document or other graphic item.

Good graphic design organizes the components of a page and makes it easy for the reader to read and understand the information on the page. Page components include type, illustrations and photographs. Graphic designers design business documents, magazines, books, direct mail, space advertising, business stationery, posters and other items.

Is the Graphic Designer an Artist?

It is helpful to be an artist but it isn't a requirement. The secretary, the multilith operator or the desktop publisher can be a graphic designer.

The designer generates the *idea* and at least a rough layout. The layout can be drawn by hand with traditional tools or created on a computer with desktop or other software. The effectiveness of the design has no relationship to the method of drawing. The use of an expensive, sophisticated software program does not guarantee an effective design. Good graphic design is produced by THINKING and applying graphic design principles, skills and experience.

A skillful, experienced graphic designer can create stunning and effective design with a marker on paper compared to the creation of an ineffective design by an amateur using a sophisticated software program. The *person* makes the difference, not the tools. Of course, if the design is produced with a marker or other hand drawing instrument, it must be converted to camera-ready art with a typesetting system. It is important to remember that the professionalism and effectiveness of a graphic design is dependent on the design skills of the designer, not on the sophistication of the design tools.

THE IMPORTANCE OF GRAPHIC DESIGN

High technology has produced computers and electronic media that store and process an incomprehensible amount of data but it has not produced the paperless office. On the contrary, computer printers annually produce more than 1,000 printed pages for every person in the United States.

Printed pages are not going to go away because people like printed pages.

Although computers are invaluable in performing many tasks electronically, they continue to produce an increasing amount of printed pages. Printed pages are not going to go away because people like printed pages. They can read them when they want to — at their own pace — and they can keep them for future use.

The problem is that the increasing number of pages generated by these computers and other methods is overwhelming the readers. And the problem is compounded by the fact that millions of these pages are ineffective, to say the least.

The reason is that armies of untrained "designers", some with aesthetic handicaps, are churning out millions of confusing, illegible documents. An over-the-shoulder peek at their computer monitor would reveal a design that looks like an electronic ransom note.

Why is this happening? Because anyone with a personal computer and a few dollars for a toy graphics software program can be, and is, a "graphic designer and typesetter" although they have no training as a graphic designer or typesetter.

Only training and experience will enable a designer to consistently produce effective pages.

Buying a violin will not make you a violinist. Buying a scalpel will not make you a neurosurgeon and buying a desktop graphics program will not make you a graphic designer or a typesetter. Only training and experience will enable a "designer" to consistently produce effective pages for the reader.

Many people think that a graphic designer simply pushes type and illustrations around a page until it looks o.k. and thereby creates a good design. Many untrained "designers" *do* create designs this way. They may even generate a pleasing layout but in most cases it is not an effective document. A successful document is produced when the designer performs the preliminary work required before designing. This includes finding out and understanding the document *message*, the profile of the reader, the available resources, the budget and the deadline.

DEVELOPMENT OF GRAPHIC DESIGN AS AN OCCUPATION

Until the fifteenth century, all books and documents were laboriously handwritten by scribes. They were the earliest graphic designers. They designed the page and produced them by handwriting. In the 1440's, German metalsmith Johann Gutenberg invented movable metal type, one of the most significant developments in history. This provided the means to produce multiple copies of books and documents by printing instead of handwriting each individual page.

As printing proliferated and spread throughout the world, a division of printing labor was generated. Graphic designers designed the page, typesetters set the page and printers printed the page.

The term "graphic designer" was coined in 1922 by William Addison Dwiggins, an American book designer. Although the term "graphic designer" wasn't used until 1922, samples of graphic design can be traced as far back as the Phoenicians who used graphic representation of language during the second millenium B.C.

As the use of the written word became widespread, the need for effective organization of the elements on a page created a need for design and graphic designers. Even in early times when documents were handwritten, scribes used a grid system to organize the text and elements of the page. To this day, publications are designed with a grid system, which will be described in other chapters of this book. Publications designed by *trained* graphic designers are designed with a grid system.

With the development of affordable personal computers and the explosion in desktop, word processing, illustration and other graphics software, almost everyone is in a position to be a graphics designer and typesetter. The objective of this book is to help improve the effectiveness of documents by providing the originator with the basics of graphic design.

GRAPHIC DESIGN TOOLS AND PROCEDURES — THE EVOLUTION

The early graphic designers used rules, calipers and engraving knives to create their designs. More recently and until the advent of computer design, graphic designers used these kinds of tools:

- Drawing boards / Line-up Tables
- T-Squares / Drafting Machines
- Markers and Marker Layout Pads
- Pens, Pencils, Scissors and X-Acto Knives
- Rubber Cement and Waxers
- Inch and Pica Rulers
- Typeface Specimen Books
- Clipper Art and Clipper Photo
- Idea (Swipe) Files and Reference Books

Of course, many designers still use these traditional tools to produce graphic designs. Not everyone is glued to a computer.

Designers using computers range from award-winning professionals to untrained, converted office personnel who are feverishly producing mountains of electronic ransom notes.

Although many sophisticated graphics software programs are available, computer "designers" use an amazing variety of software programs, some of which were written for non-graphic applications. This is one of the reasons why an understanding of graphics is invaluable – so the designer can apply graphic design principles and concepts regardless of the software program being used.

PRE-DESIGN REQUIREMENTS

Without a goal, how would you know when you get there?

Effective graphic design begins with pre-design planning. The writing of a report begins with an outline and the building of a house begins with a blueprint. The design of a document begins with a goal and planning. Without a goal, how would you know when you get there?

The mark of an amateur is the creation of a design without a goal and planning. These pre-design requirements are described in detail in Chapter Two, *Pre-Design Planning for Effective Documents.*

Graphic design in a sixteenth-century printer's shop.

Graphic design using a computer and a software program.

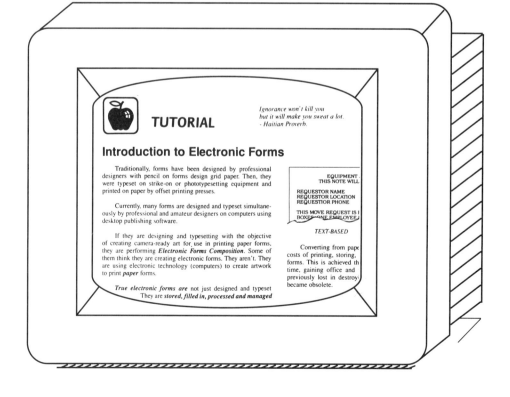

If you don't know
what your objectives are,
how will you know
when you get there?

Chapter Two
Pre-Design Planning for Effective Documents

Ignorance doesn't kill you,
but it makes you
sweat a lot.

— Haitian Proverb

2 Pre-Design Planning for Effective Documents

DESIGNING TO MEET THE OBJECTIVE

Amateur desktop publishers are so fascinated with their electronic tools they spend more time with graphic embellishments than they do with the document message and contents.

The first step in effective design is to determine the objective, the *purpose* of the design. The designer needs to be more than hands on a keyboard or a twitchy finger on a mouse.

Only by idenifying the objective can you focus on designing an effective page.

The objective may be to sell a product or service, to get employees to attend a company picnic, to raise money or to influence opinion. The objective may be to sell, identify, inform or to gather information. Only by identifying the objective can you focus on designing an effective page.

For example, if the objective of a flyer is to get as many employees as possible to attend the company picnic, you need to focus on the *reasons* why they should attend. People attend picnics to relax and have fun. They go to enjoy food and drink, to play games and to enjoy the company of their fellow employees. Therefore, the headline, the illustrations and the text should focus on the reasons why they should attend the picnic.

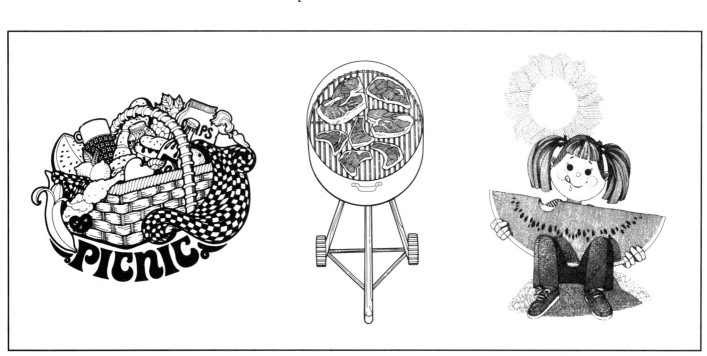

DESIGNING FOR THE READER

The designer must also consider the reader. Who is the message aimed at? Identifying readers helps you choose techniques that engage them. Are they colleagues, clients, prospects, senior citizens, children or college instructors? What do they have in common?

Focusing on the reader helps the graphic designer make decisions about the style, the language, the typefaces and the general tone of the document. For example, senior citizens need larger type and college instructors need an approach different than elementary school pupils. Instruction manuals should contain headlines, sub-heads and graphic devices to help the reader find and understand what they need to know.

Identifying readers helps you create a design that engages them.

WHAT INFORMATION MUST BE INCLUDED?

Different documents have different elements. A book needs a preface, an index and perhaps a glossary and a bibliography. A direct mail ad may need a headline, an offer, a description of the product or service, a price and an order form. A form may have a title, a form number, instructions, an introduction, a body and a closing section.

The designer can't make an intelligent design without an understanding of each of the elements required for a document.

The designer can't make an intelligent design without an understanding of the elements required for a particular document. The designer must provide appropriate space for each element and insure that they are in the proper sequence.

THE APPROPRIATE IMAGE MUST BE PROJECTED

Everything (typefaces, illustrations, photos, paper, ink, color, etc.) contributes to the image that a document conveys about the originator. The design should convey an image that is appropriate for the document message and the reader.

The projected image for a memorial service program would be formal and dignified. The projected image for a travel brochure would be adventurous.

The typeface selection is particularly important. The type must match and reinforce the message. The appropriate typeface strengthens the message while inappropriate type weakens the message and confuses the reader.

Appropriate Type

Inappropriate Type

Must the Design Conform to a Corporate Standard or Be Consistent with a Series of Documents?

Most corporations develop and implement graphic standards with the objective of projecting a chosen, consistent corporate image. The corporate standards include logo guides and may also include type, typography, color, paper, ink and other graphic standards. Corporate standards are increasingly important due to the proliferation of decentralized desktop publishing and the opportunity for uncontrolled corporate document "creativity".

Desktop publishers may feel that corporate standards cramp their style but actually it helps by letting them concentrate on the *contents* of the document.

If the document is part of a series of documents, a consistent design should be established for all documents in the series. For example, the design for all corporate stationery (letterheads, envelopes, monarch-size letterheads and envelopes, inter-office memos, fax cover sheets, business cards, etc.) should have a unifying, consistent design. Consistent design should also be employed for other series of documents like newsletters and special project reports.

Desktop publishers may feel that corporate standards cramp their style but actually it helps by letting them concentrate on the contents of the document.

THE DESIGNER MUST CONSIDER BUDGET LIMITATIONS

The amount of money that can be spent on the document affects the method of reproduction and consequently, the design itself. Is the designer limited to black ink or is spot color or full color an option? Will it be reproduced on an office copier or an offset press? Can the designer use photographs, reverses, variable screens, diecutting, scoring, punching or other features? Will the camera-ready copies be produced on 300 dpi laser printers or high resolution imagesetters?

The answers to these kinds of questions will determine what features and techniques are available to the designer for a particular document.

THE DEADLINE CAN AFFECT THE DESIGN

The longer the deadline the more time you have to create an interesting, effective design. Conversely, the tighter the deadline, the less time there is to work on the design. Usually, tight deadlines produce simpler designs.

Performing the pre-design planning described in this chapter will help you to design effective documents.

Chapter Three
Principles of Graphic Design

*Every artist was first
an amateur.*

— *Ralph Waldo Emerson*

3 Principles of Graphic Design

PROVIDE INSTANTLY UNDERSTANDABLE COMMUNICATIONS

The reader does not want to have to fight to understand your document. The reader is already bombarded with an overwhelming amount of visual messages (mail, junk mail, fax, junk fax, forms, reports, newsletters, computer catalogs, billboards, traffic signs, T-shirts, etc.).

The reader doesn't want to have to fight to understand your message.

Unless there is an urgent need, the reader does not want to read boring documents or ones with a message that can't be understood with one glance. So, don't be too intellectual when you are designing. The objective is to present a clear, easily understood message, not to impress the reader with your sophistication and keen insight into the mysteries of the universe.

Headlines and graphic devices such as illustrations and photographs related to the message, are useful in providing instantly understandable communications. For example, the "SLEEP CHEAP" billboard for the Red Roof budget hotel chain provides instant understandable communication. Another example is a full color photograph of a sizzling steak at the top of a menu. It says more than the words below it.

This famous headline provided instantly understandable communication. The graphics are not impressive but this ad, written in December, 1936, sold one million books in three years. It was an advertising landmark of the Thirties.

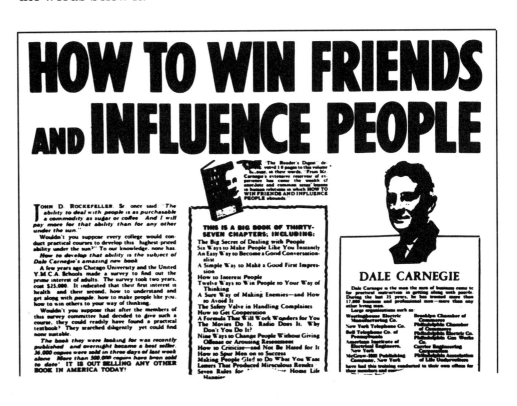

The designer can also improve communication by providing precise titles for business documents like reports and forms. Approximately one-fourth of all business documents are forms. All forms should have titles that describe the function of the form. "Supplies Sheet" is not a good title because it doesn't describe the function of the form to the reader. A better title would be "Request for Office Supplies".

To summarize, arrange the page so the reader with one glance, can understand the message. Don't make the reader fight to grasp the message.

USE AN APPROPRIATE ALIGNMENT SYSTEM

Almost every document must be designed with some kind of alignment system. It provides an organization and an order required for the reader to understand the message and feel comfortable with the page.

Alignment systems are either symmetrical (centered) or asymmetrical (off-centered). The choice between centered or off-centered is an important decision for the designer because the alignment system impacts the reader. It sets the tone of the document.

Symmetrical Alignment

Generally, a symmetrical (centered) design is formal, conservative and restful. It is usually used for items like wedding invitations, theatre programs and letterheads for attorneys. It is easy to use and always works. It usually doesn't create an exciting or brilliant design although it is certainly possible that an imaginative designer can use it to create a exciting design.

An excellent technique for improving a centered layout is to arrange the page elements in a geometric pattern, as shown in the illustration.

When using a centered alignment, the design will look better if the widest lines are near the top. The overall image should look more like an inverted triangle than one with the base at the bottom.

Generally, it is not a good idea to mix symmetrical and asymmetrical alignments on the same document. They usually conflict and destroy the tone of the document.

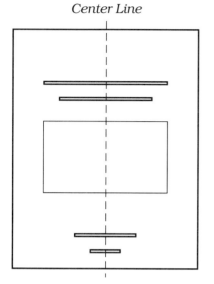

Center Line

A layout with symmetrical (centered) alignment.

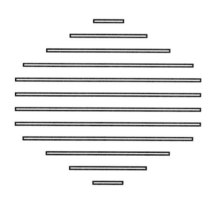

A centered layout in a geometric pattern.

A symmetrical (centered) design is usually used for formal, conservative items like invitations.

You are cordially invited to a party celebrating the divorce of the former Mr. and Mrs. Jack Spratt

To accommodate friends of both antagonists, high cholesterol and also fat free hors doeuvre's will be served.

Asymmetrical Alignment

An asymmetrical alignment is not centered. If the design is folded vertically it does not create a mirror image. Generally, it is not formal or conservative. It usually creates more interest and can be dramatic and exciting. Common asymmetrical alignments are described below.

Flush Left

Flush Left

Flush left, also called "flush left, ragged right", is an excellent choice for many, if not most documents. It is a natural and intuitive alignment since it conforms to the way people read (in our culture). It also retains proper word spacing since spaces are not altered to force right hand justification, as they are in justified alignment.

The word "justified" also called "right justified" refers to text that is aligned on the left and the right. If the entire page is justified, it is basically a centered layout although sections of justified type can be placed on an off-centered page.

Flush Right

Flush right alignment, as shown in the illustration, is not used as often as some of the other alignment methods. Although it is used infrequently, some designs do call for its use and the designer should have flush right alignment in his/her repertoire.

Diagonal Alignment

Diagonal alignment is attention-getting and dynamic. Diagonal alignment can be used for one or a few words or elements or for an entire page.

If course, this dynamic alignment system can only be used for dynamic documents. It wouldn't thrill the survivors who are reading a memorial service program.

Flush Right

Diagonal alignment is attention-getting and dynamic.

DETERMINE THE IMPORTANCE OF EACH DESIGN ELEMENT AND GIVE THEM EACH THE PROPER VISUAL STRENGTH

Effective design isn't produced by moving headlines, text and illustrations around until they look good. The designer must understand the document objective and determine the dominant element, other important elements and subordinate elements. Only then can the proper elements be emphasized by using a large size, color or other highlighting technique. The emphasized elements must reinforce the message. You don't emphasize elements for graphic considerations.

Avoid "too equal" emphasis and divisions of space. Allocate space in relation to the importance of the design elements.

Contrast is the key to successful layouts. The important elements should be significantly bigger or stronger visually in contrast to the less important elements.

(Headline – 2nd Most Important Element)

HEADLINE

(Text – Subordinate Element)

Photo (Most Important Element)

The layout lacks contrast. It doesn't signal the important items to the reader.

In this re-design of the layout on the left the important elments are emphasized by enlarging them. The contrast also adds interest to the page.

GROUP DESIGN ELEMENTS INTO EASY-TO-READ CHUNKS

Readers will try to avoid pages that are not broken into easy-to-read chunks. The designer should group elements into short chunks surrounded by white frames of space. If your page looks like the white pages of the telephone directory the reader will read it only if it is urgent.

Avoid the "white pages" look. Divide your page into easy-to-read chunks.

```
SPIVAK Ben 95 Cableknoll Ln ------ 360-9016
  Bronya 1500 Warrensville Center Rd -- 291-8958
  E 4559 Lander Rd ------------ 248-2927
  F 14400 Cedar Rd ----------- 382-0572
  Richard B 95 Cableknoll Ln ---- 360-9006
SPIVERY Curtis 18049 Nancy Dr ---- 692-1964
  W C 3928 Lancaster Rd ------- 531-6559
SPIVEY A B 17105 Lomond Bl ------ 751-4759
  Alan D 1449 Ridgewood Av ----- 529-0619
  Alvin 3567 E 138 St --------- 752-4517
  Arlene 14904 Thames Av ------ 851-0862
  B A 17460 Chagrin Bl -------- 491-9316
  Chas 4780 Henry St --------- 581-2331
  D 13945 Superior Rd -------- 371-8879
  Darrell H 872 Nela View Rd---- 541-6024
  E W 3341 Berkeley Av -------- 932-9074
  Geneva 1138 E 78 St -------- 391-8205
  J R 19761 Locherie Av ------ 531-2659
  John Y 3187 Ashwood Rd ------ 751-4154
  L 1575 East Bl ------------ 791-5737
  Lawrence 683 E 115 St ------ 761-0687
  Randy 9511 Benham Av ------- 883-4108
  S A 3277 E 143 St --------- 561-8328
  T 15601 Judson Dr --------- 921-9280
  T 1292 E 134 St ---------- 541-3246
SPIVY M ---------------- 731-1059
SPIWAK R 2020 Taylor Rd -------- 451-5155
  Robt Al 8713 Morton Av ------ 661-7721
   M C 2542 E 127 St -    -- 421-6858

SPONSELLER A 20090 Laverne Av ---- 333-6576
  Alan W 24261 Mastick Rd ------- 777-3981
  B 4449 W 53 St ----------- 741-4657
  David J 10183 Hickory Ridge Dr -- 546-0414
  E 6805 Mayfield Rd -------- 646-0677
  Elmer J 12700 Lake Av ------- 221-9191
  Gregory atty 43 E Bridge St ----- 826-4114
  Gregory M 664 Tauton Dr ------ 234-1885
  Gregory M atty 1 Cleveland Center -- 781-4112
  H J 525 Button Rd --------- 232-9361
  J 1569 Lauderdale Av ------ 226-6985
  J 5932 Stumph Rd---------- 884-7651
  Jerry 14011 Brookpark Rd------ 267-2916
  Jerry E 22252 Crestridge Dr ----- 243-5078
  John 3130 W 160 St -------- 228-8583
  Richard Lee 5915 Dorothy Dr ---- 779-9264
  Vernon 28438 Elder Dr -------- 235-5615
SPONSLER Kenneth 92 Egbert Rd --- 439-4665
SPONTELLI Beverly A 5415 Warwick Dr 888-8726
  Chas A 6203 Dawn Vista Oval ----- 886-5964
  Frank 13455 Laurel Ln -------- 328-0946
  Leonard 981 E Dartmoor Av ----- 524-5572
  Nathan 4806 Behrwald Av ------ 741-1358
  Nick 7003 Night Vista Dr ------ 842-5577
SPONZA Bernardo 4388 Tamalga Dr -- 381-7034
SPOON Jas 638 E 128 St ------- 681-6820
  Max H 2077 W 32 St -------- 281-7626
  Murray 1620 Bryn Mawr Rd ----- 249-9403
  V I 1867 Taylor Rd ---------- 761-1203

  S 15117 Edgewater Dr -
  Wilbur F 13431 Lake Av
SPOTZ Daniel 20511 Fuller
  Darren 1540 Lee Terrace D.
  Richard T Jr atty Hunting
SPRACHMANN K 3566 W 1
SPRADLIN Scott & Julia
  25820 Highland Rd --
SPRADLING Clarence
  David 8992 Ridgewoo.
  M 8659 N Akins Rd --
SPRAFKA Frank 1600 Mall.
  Jos S 440 E 329 St ----
  Kimberly 358 E 288 St --
SPRAGGE A E 1604 Winche'
SPRAGGINS C 20827 Lora'
  E 5653 Adams Av ----
  Elmer 2552 Chestnut Rd
  Geo A 13204 Orme Rd --
  J 19098 Westwood Dr --
  Jeff 12114 Havana Rd --
  L 1360 E 88 St -----
  Lawrence 5911 Oakes R
  Leroy 2224 E 85 St ----
  Mamie 10808 Greenlawn
  R 10324 Sandusky Av ---
  Wayne G 14801 Kennerdow
  Willie S 1066 Carlyon Rd -
```

In this layout, the reader is overwhelmed by solid text. There is no rest for the eye.

11 Designing Unit Sets, Continuous and Specialty Forms

INTRODUCTION TO SPECIALTY FORMS

To increase the speed and efficiency of data entry and forms processing, designers have created many types of time-saving specialty forms.

Forms design principles for specialty forms are basically the same for cut sheets. The difference is in the *construction* of specialty forms. This difference requires the designer to understand the printing method and the construction because it affects the design.

For example, the *basic design* of a unit set is the same as it is for a cut sheet. The difference is that for a unit set, the designer must know standard unit set sizes (which are different than cut sheet sizes), stub locations and sizes, lock-up requirements, carbon paper and carbonless paper standards, etc.

Sometimes novice designers become so involved in specialty form construction they forget the basic forms design principles. Like cut sheets, unit sets and other specialty forms should have a form title, form number, form zones and comply with other forms design principles.

MATERIALS USED TO CONSTRUCT SPECIALTY FORMS

The primary materials used to construct specialty forms are form bond paper, ink, carbon paper and carbonless paper. A wide variety of these materials are available and the proper selection of them for a business form is vital to the efficiency of that form.

For example, if you can't read the information on part 4 of a unit set because of poor paper and carbon paper selection, the form doesn't have much value, although it may have a good appearance.

Form Bond Paper

Most specialty forms are printed on form bond paper. This type of paper has good printing qualities and good writing and handling qualities. Form bond is produced in white and colors and the basic sheet size is 17" x 22". Rolls of form bond for producing specialty forms like unit sets and continuous forms normally are manufactured in diameter from 28" to 60". [...] form bond is manufact[...]

This layout is more appealing to the reader because it is broken into easy-to-read chunks.

USE WHITE SPACE AS A DESIGN ELEMENT

Use white space to display other elements on the page.

One of the biggest design problems is the improper use of white space. White space is a design element. It shouldn't be considered as something that is left over after the important elements are placed on the page. White space should be a positive element, not a negative item in the background.

It is helpful to think of white space as a layout tool. Don't be afraid to use white space. Use it to display the other elements on the page to their best advantage. Readers won't complain of wasted space but they will complain about crowded pages that are difficult to read.

White space is most effective if it has a *clearly defined geometric shape*. White space shouldn't be randomly dispersed. Group it into large geometric shapes. It should have a planned shape and location on the page. Use it to frame elements on the page. If used properly, it is effective and it is inexpensive.

Readers won't complain about "wasted" white space. They will complain about crowded pages that are difficult to read.

White space is most effective if it has a clearly defined geometric shape.

Chapter Four

Type – The Key Element
in Graphic Design

*Type and graphic design
have been around a lot longer
than desktop publishing.*

4

Type – The Key Element in Graphic Design

TYPE – AN OVERVIEW

Type is the key element in graphic design. Illustrations, photographs, symbols and other elements do not appear in every graphic document but type is present in almost every document.

Type is the only element that is present on almost every graphic page.

There are thousands of typefaces available and an infinite number of ways they can be used on a page. The possibilities are limitless and can be overwhelming to the novice designer. Type is complicated. You won't learn everything about type from this chapter, another book or a desktop software manual. The best teacher is experience.

If you're a type "dummy" this chapter will help you with the basics and the language. It will help you choose appropriate typefaces and show you how type is used on the page.

THE SIGNIFICANCE OF TYPE

The invention of movable type by Johann Gutenberg was one of the most important developments in history. It provided the means for the spread of information to the entire world. The objective of good typography is to provide clear, easily understood printed communication. Design based on graphic aesthetics is important but the emphasis should be on clearly communicating the document *message.*

The invention of movable type by Johann Gutenberg provided the means for the spread of information to the entire world.

The *content* should control design, not the graphics or the technology. The designer must first read and understand the *message* before attempting the design. The designer must thoroughly understand the meaning to ensure that the document is logically organized and that the important elements are highlighted by priority.

Readers only want information that is easy to read, understand and use. They don't care how the document was produced. They don't care if you used a Macintosh or a PC clone made in Bangladesh. And they don't care if you used a word processing program, a presentation program or page make-up software. To them the technology is irrelevant.

Communication is not machine-specific. The designer's job is to ensure that the document's message jumps off the page and into the reader's mind, regardless of the technology used to produce the page. Although technology's tools are amazing and typography can approach an art form, the objective is to achieve effective communication.

TYPE DEFINITIONS

Typeface

A typeface is a family of letters and characters of a consistent design. The term "face" originally referred to the surface of a piece of metal type.

The name of this typeface is ITC Garamond Bold

Font

A font contain all the characters of a particular typeface. It can include uppercase letters, lowercase letters, punctuation marks, figures and symbols.

ITC Garamond Bold

abcdefghijklmnopqrstuvwxyz
ABCDEFGHIJKLMNOPQRSTUVWXYZ&
1234567890.,:;"!?¢$

Type Family

A type family consist of a group of fonts such as regular, light, bold, italic, condensed and expanded faces.

Type Style

Type style refers to the variation of shapes and thicknesses within a typeface. Type styles can be light, bold, italic or consist of other variations of a particular typeface. The designer uses various type styles within a typeface to provide interest and to highlight important words. The use of various type styles help clarify the document's message and adds contrast and interest. Usually, the designer can find enough styles within one typeface to get across the message for a particular document.

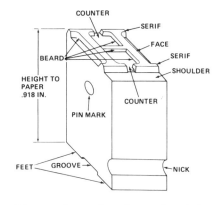

The surface of a piece of metal type was called a "face". This is the origin of the word "typeface".

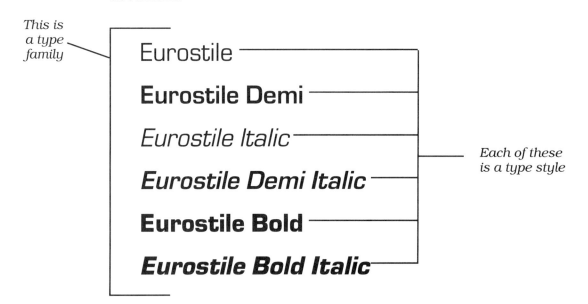

This is a type family

Eurostile

Eurostile Demi

Eurostile Italic

Eurostile Demi Italic

Eurostile Bold

Eurostile Bold Italic

Each of these is a type style

Type Provides Endless Opportunities

Type can be used to inform, entertain and create feelings and moods. Type can be elegant, exciting, loud, soft, masculine, feminine, friendly, threatening and ugly.

And whether intentional or unintentional, type on the printed page can be amusing. Just take a look at these typographical errors and bloopers.

To the ringing cry of "Hi-yo Silver!" the Lone Banger rides again.
(TV Guide)

Lettuce won't turn brown if you put your head in a plastic bag before placing it in the refrigerator.
(London Daily Mail-Eng.)

As an encore, Miss Davis played the old favorite "Carry Me Back to Old Virginity."
(Winfield Courier-Kan.)

Ringling Bros. Circus advertising for an understudy for the human cannon ball: Must be willing to travel.
(Orlando Sentinel-Fla.)

After returning from their African safari, the two men showed their guests the many interesting photos of the large breasts they had found in the jungle.
(Tampa Tribune-Fla.)

FIVE SCHOOL BROADS APPROVE SEX EDUCATION
(Raleigh News & Observer-N.C.)

We are happy to announce the engagement of Gene Kelly to Prince Rainier. He will now become a Princess.
(New York Times)

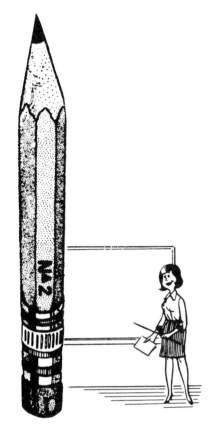

Contest rules are that snapshots must be of a person not larger than 8 x 10 inches.

Muskogee Times – Democrat - Okla.

SELECTING TYPE TO FIT THE JOB

Selection of an appropriate typeface for a document is vital to the effectiveness of the document. The typeface must match the character of the document. If it does, it will enhance the success of the document. If it doesn't match, it will impair the character of the document.

Considering the multitude of available typefaces, selection of an appropriate face can be bewildering. If you don't have a lot of experience, scanning a type specimen list until you find an interesting face is not a good solution.

Typeface Classification

Almost all typefaces can be identified as serif or sans serif. The main classification of typefaces is determined by whether a letter has serifs or not. Serifs are the finishing strokes (lines or curves) at the

Serif Type

Sans-serif Type

top and bottom of a letter. Typefaces without serifs are called sans serif faces. Sans comes from the French and means "without".

Serif faces are also sometimes called Roman faces because serifs appeared as marks made by chiseling letters into Roman monuments.

Serif typefaces were the earliest typefaces. Sans serif faces are a more recent development. Throughout the history of typesetting and printing serif faces have been used for setting text (paragraphs). The horizontal serifs help the eye to read along the horizontal lines of type in text. Readability studies have generally supported the theory that serif typefaces are easier to read in text form.

The basic decision in selecting an appropriate typeface is to choose either a serif or a sans serif face. Serif faces make one think of earlier times and formality. Serif type is also used for long passages of text, as found in books, magazines newspapers and newsletters.

Sans serif faces makes one think of informality and are often used for modern themes and shorter text and headlines.

Common uses for serif type

Many paragraphs of text

Lorem ipsum dolor sit amet, consectetur adips aliquam erat volupat. Ut enim ad minimim ve commodo consequat. Duis autem vel eum inu dolore eu fugiat nulla pariatur. At vero eos et a et molestais ex ceptur sint occeacat cupidat norn dolor fugi. Et harumd dereud facilis est er exp impedit anim id quad maxium placeat facer i quinsud et aur office debit aut tum rerum nec rerum hic tenetury sapiente delectus au aut pr ne ad eam non possing accommodare nost ri accese potest giesr ad augendas cum consci modut est neque nonor imper ned ilbiding adithd inflammad ut coercend magist and et doder

Formal Message

Greene and Speaker
Attorneys at Law
123 Trial Lane
Cleveland, OH 44115

Common uses for sans serif type

Headlines and a few lines of text

BIG SANS SERIF HEADLINE

Sub-Head

Lorem ipsum dolor sit amet, cosectetur adip nonnumy eiusmod tempor incidunt ut labore erat volupat. Ut enim ad minimim veniami quis

Sub-Head

ullamcorpor suscipit lbaoris nisi ut aliquidp ex Duis autem vel eum irare dolor in reprehende

Informal Message

Computer Discount , Inc.
123 Hard Drive
Silicon, CA 94512

After the basic decision of serif or sans serif is made, the designer must choose among the various serif or sans serif faces that are available. After reading the rest of this chapter it will be easier to make that decision.

The reader is not impressed by type that is difficult to read.

Legibility – The First Factor in Selecting Typefaces

Type is meant to be read. The reader is not impressed by novelty type that can't be read. The first factor in choosing type is legibility. The typeface should be easy to read. Your objective is not to choose the weirdest typefaces you can find. Your objective is to choose *legible* typefaces that are appropriate for the subject matter.

Choose legible typefaces like these

New Century Schoolbook Roman   Times Roman

Helvetica Medium   **Souvenir Demi**

Typefaces like these are not as legible.

In addition to choosing legible typefaces, you need to ensure readability by making sure the type:

1. Is big enough to read.
2. Is set in a line length that is not too long or too short.
3. Provides a contrast to the background.

You won't be able to read the most legible type in the world if you print it with dark blue ink on a dark blue background or if you print it in yellow ink on a white background. *Contrast* is necessary for readability.

Also, to increase readability and avoid the appearance of a ransom note, use the least possible number of typefaces on a page. Usually, you can get the typographic variety you need by using the various styles (bold, italic, etc.) and sizes available from only one type family. It's a good idea to stick to one family until you get more experience in choosing typefaces.

Selecting Typefaces to Match the Job

The typeface must be compatible with the words and the message. Every typeface has a unique personality, an appearance that makes it suited for a particular document. Type can be feminine, masculine, friendly, harsh, elegant, delicate, old-fashioned, modern, etc. The challenge is to select a typeface that matches the document content and is also legible and readable when it appears in the format you will use on your design.

The beginning designer can start out by choosing Times Roman for serif applications (formal & conservative content and long text passages) and Helvetica for informal, modern content. Times Roman and Helvetica are so popular they are clichés but they work. Later, other typefaces can be chosen that more closely match the content of the document.

When choosing appropriate typefaces, it can be helpful to first generate adjectives that describe the mood or feeling that you want achieved – adjectives like masculine, strong, elegant, romantic, friendly and dramatic. Then choose a typeface with a personality that matches the adjective(s). Make sure it is legible.

If you were designing a brochure describing bulldozing, equipment you would not use a thin elegant type. Naturally, you would use a bold, strong type. If the brochure described women's lingerie, you would use a delicate, feminine typeface. Although these examples are obvious, the same principles can be applied to other documents.

Feminine
Garamond Book Italic

Masculine
Futura Extra Bold

Friendly
Souvenir Demi

Elegant
Garamond Book

Old-Fashioned
𝕷𝔦𝔫𝔬𝔱𝔢𝔵𝔱

BULLDOZER *(Appropriate)*

Bulldozer *(Inappropriate)*

LACE DOILIES *(Inappropriate)*

Lace Doilies *(Appropriate)*

Times Roman

The most popular serif typeface.

Helvetica

The most popular sans serif typeface.

The selected typeface must also be compatible with the illustrations and the photos on the page. They must all look like they like each other. If they look like they are afraid of each other, choose a different typeface. Type is more visual than intellectual. If it looks right, it's right! If it doesn't look right, it isn't right. End of story.

And don't forget that type, illustrations and photos can be integrated. They can be friendly and perhaps even intimate. They can touch and even overlap.

TYPE BASICS

Language and Anatomy

Type has been around for hundreds of years. To fully understand the language, anatomy and basics of type would take a lot of reading and a lot of experience. The language alone contains words like posture, measure, muts, ems, quads, ens, nut quads and nuts — not to mention picas, points, kerning, x-heights, counters, ascenders and fillets.

Upper Case

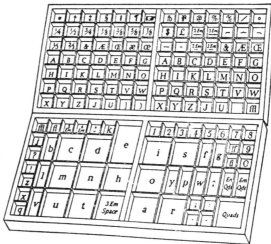
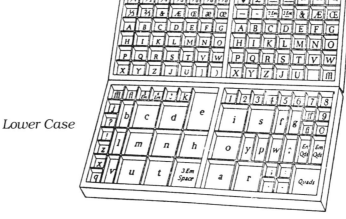

Lower Case

Type was organized in compartments as shown. The terms "uppercase" and "lowercase" were derived from this method of storing type in cases. Each piece of type in the case was called a sort. If you emptied one of the compartments in the case, you were "out of sorts".

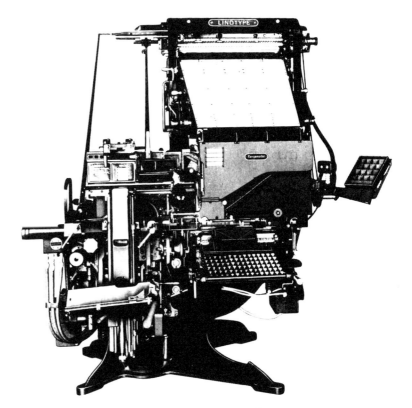

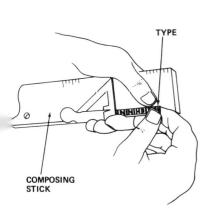

TYPE

COMPOSING
STICK

A composing stick used to assemble foundry type.

Mergenthaler Linotype Machine

There are entire books written about the language, anatomy and basics of type. Most of them would put you to sleep even if you were reading them while reclining on a barbed-wire fence. You can probably get by without muts and nuts but it would be helpful if you knew a little about the basics of type.

Type Family

A type family includes all the variations of a single typeface. These variations (styles) have different weights, slants and widths. Some families have many styles and some do not. Helvetica is a sample of a family with many styles.

Helvetica Family
(Some teenagers and uncles are missing)

Some typeface families have many styles and some families have as few as two styles.

Helvetica Light
Helvetica Light Oblique
Helvetica
Helvetica Italic
Helvetica Bold
Helvetica Bold Italic
Helvetica Condensed
Helvetica Condensed Oblique
Helvetica Condensed Bold
Helvetica Condensed Bold Oblique
Helvetica Black
Helvetica Black Oblique

Anatomy of Type

Here are some of the basic anatomical terms.

The point size is the vertical distance from the top of the ascenders to the bottom of the descenders.

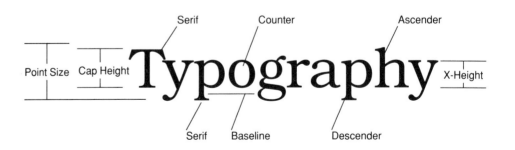

Ascenders are the parts of lowercase letters that extend up above the waist line. *Descenders* are the parts of letter that extend down below the baseline. X-height is the vertical dimension between the waist line and the baseline.

Type Size

Type is also classified by size. Larger type (generally 18 points and above) is called display type or headline type. Smaller type is called body type because it is used in the body of a document. Smaller type is also called text type.

Before desktop publishing, display type was generally set in sizes from 18 to 72 points (about one inch high). Now much taller letterforms are available but there are still few occasions where 10-inch high type is required.

The classic size for body type is 10 point with 12 point leading. Larger body type can look gaudy and overdone and smaller body type is difficult for some people to read.

The type size (also referred to as point size or type height) is measured in points. There are 72 points per inch. There are 12 points in a pica and six picas to an inch (not exactly, but close enough for working purposes). In copymarking, points are designated by the initial "pt.", as in 10 pt.

The point size of a typeface is calculated by measuring the vertical distance from the tops of ascenders to the bottoms of the descenders. Although the distance between ascenders and descenders, among typefaces in the same point size, is the same, their differing x-heights will cause some faces to *appear* larger or smaller than others.

Since points are the smallest unit of measurement, they are used to measure the height of type. Picas are the larger unit of measurement and used to describe the length of the line. Picas are written "pi". A line measuring 24 picas is written x24 and is read "by 24".

Generally, type that is 18 points and above is called display type or headline type. Smaller type is called body type or text type.

The classic size for body type is 10 point with 12 point leading.

Points are used to measure the height of type and picas are used to measure line lengths.

This is 6 point type

This is 10 point type

This is 18 point type

This is 24 point type

This is 36 point type

Although for practical purposes, desktop publishers say that a pica is one-sixth of an inch and that there are six picas to an inch, it isn't true. Six picas are .9961 inch. For distances under about 10 inches, it doesn't make much difference, but on larger distances, the discrepancy is noticeable. This is particularly important in forms typesetting, especially machine written forms, because these machines space in inches, not picas.

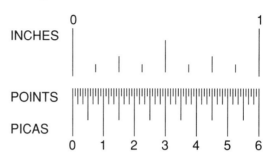

There are 12 points to a pica and almost 6 picas to an inch (72 points to an inch).

Weight and Posture

Type families come in variations of weight and posture. Weight refers to the thickness of lines that form a letter. The weights range from light to bold. Some typeface families exist in a wide variety of weights while others have only a few weight varieties. No typeface offers every weight and weights in different type families are not consistent.

Posture refers to the *angle* of the type — vertical or slanted to the right. Vertical is also referred to as "Roman". There are two kinds of slanted type, italic and oblique. Italic type is not only slanted, it is a different font. It was designed to highlight words when used in a type family with regular vertical type. An example is Times Roman Italic which is used with Times Roman type.

Oblique type is created by slanting regular type which remains unchanged in other respects.

Italic type is not only slanted, it is a different font.

ITALIC

Medium/Vertical

Italic

Bold Italic

OBLIQUE

Medium/Vertical

Oblique

Bold Oblique

Oblique type is created electronically by slanting regular vertical type. It is unchanged in other respects.

When copymarking, write the weight and posture after the name of the typeface. For example, 12-point Bookman Bold Italic.

It is important to remember that different weights of the same family in the same point size will occupy different lines lengths. For example, bold always takes more left to right space than medium type.

Typeface Variations

In addition to the type basics already described, the designer needs to be familiar with type variations. With desktop publishing, there is virtually no limit to electronic distortion and variation of type. Listed below are some of the common variations.

There is virtually no limit to typeface variations.

CONDENSED	Type is condensed when its width is reduced without reducing its height. Condensed type can be set from a condensed font or be created by electronic manipulation.
EXPANDED	Type is expanded when its width is increased without increasing its height. Expanded type can be set from an expanded font or be created by electronic manipulation.
REVERSE TYPE	Reverse type is usually white type on a black or dark background
OUTLINE	Outline type is used occasionally for contrast or highlighting. It is difficult to read and not effective in smaller point sizes.
Shadow	Shadow type is created by offsetting one typeface style on another style. Shadow type is more effective in larger point sizes.
50% Screened Type	Screened type is created by filling the letterform with small dots instead of solid black. Screened type is also more effective in larger point sizes.
Projected Up Right	Projected type is used sometimes for attention-getting. It's an impressive term to use in conversations around the water cooler.
15° Right Skewed Type 15° Left Skewed Type	Skewed type is slanted, either to the right or to the left. If it is skewed to the right, it is called oblique and is generally not skewed more than 15%. Don't skew to the left. People don't like it.
20° Rotated Type Counterclockwise	The baseline of rotated type is at an angle — not the usual horizontal.

Since there virtually are no limits to typeface variation, it is important to remember that some variations are not easy to read. It is vital to choose readable type.

Line Length and Leading

The line length (measure) of the column to the right ➡ is 31 picas.

Line length, also known as the "measure" or the column width is the length of a line or the width of a block of body type. This length is expressed in picas.

Leading is the term used for line spacing, the vertical distance between the baselines of type. Leading is pronounced "Ledd-ing" and originated from the practice of inserting strips of lead metal between lines of metal type, to spread the spacing between the lines. If type is set "solid", the leading (in points) is the same as the point size of the type. If the type size is nine points and the leading is 10 points, the lines will be leaded 1 point. Generally, adding a point or two leading to body type increases readability.

This type is set "solid", 10-point type and 10-point leading.

This same 10-point type is set 12-points between baselines. It is leaded 2 points.

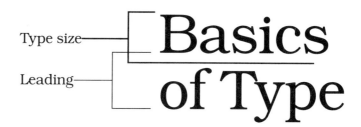

Type size
Leading

Without leading it can be difficult for the eye to scan the line because there is no significant band of white space to guide it from left to right. If there is too much leading, the eye is overpowered by big bands of horizontal white space. The classic typeface, point size and leading for text is 10/12 Times Roman Medium. The point size and leading are read as "10 on 12".

This is 10/12 Times Roman Medium, the classic typeface, point size and leading.

Letterspacing and Word Spacing

Letterspacing refers to the space between letters of a line of type. Of course, each typeface has built-in letterspacing. The typeface designer built in space on the left side of the letter called left side bearing and space on the right side called right side bearing.

Most typesetting systems allow the keyboard operator to reduce or expand the built-in letterspacing to accommodate their personal taste or judgment for a particular document. It is vital to retain individual character recognition. Some designers like to set letterspacing tight while others prefer normal or open letterspacing. In addition to this decision which affects the letterspacing between all letters, certain pairs of adjacent letters require special letterspacing called kerning. Certain adjacent letters, because of their shape, have too much white space between them. Kerning is the procedure of removing space between certain letters to tighten their fit. Some examples of letter pairs that require kerning are shown in the example. Kerning allows the adjustment of the bearings of letters and improves the appearance of the line of type.

Kerning allows the adjustment of the bearings of letters and improves the appearance of the line of type.

Not Kerned ➡ AT AY AV AW LT LY

Kerned ➡ AT AY AV AW LT LY

Wordspacing refers to the spaces between words. There should be enough space between words so they can be easily recognized but not so much that the word spacing is noticeable. If there is too much word spacing, it will cause vertical white rivers running down the page which is unsightly and distracts from the horizontal eye flow.

Symbols, Bullets, Rules and Other Stuff

Type symbols not found on a normal font are called pi characters. They include legal, mathematical and multilingual symbols.

$ Dollars	@ At, apiece	™ Trademark
¢ Cents	% Percent	® Registered
£ Pounds sterling	℅ In care of	© Copyright
¥ Yen		

Sample of some symbols.

Bullets are used to highlight items in a list and to attract attention and add interest to a document. Bullets are round shaped and are either solid or open. Bullets should not be larger than the x-height of the type or they will look like bowling balls. If it is a "square bullet", it is called a ballot.

- Bullet
- Open bullet
- Ballot box
- Square bullet

In typesetting, a dingbat is not a name for an eccentric person who lives in the attic. *Dingbats* are ornamental designs that are used to attract attention to an area on a document. Dingbats can be used instead of bullets. The advantage of dingbats is that one can be selected that relates to the words or the general tone or message of the document. You can also create a message-related border by repeating the dingbat.

Dingbats

These are not "typographic" dingbats.

Most desktop software provides the availability of producing a staggering variety of rules (lines), boxes, geometric shapes and other graphics. Since they are easy to produce, there is a tendency to overuse the graphics and overwhelm the more important headlines and text. Your business report shouldn't look like a promo for Walt Disney's Fantasia.

Don't overdo graphics. If your layout looks like Walt Disney threw up on it — it's overdone.

Hairline (0.3 point)

Half point

1 point

1.5 point

2 point

3 point

4 point

6 point

8 point

10 point

Double half point

Thick-thin (2 point + half point)

Commonly used rules

Rounded-Corner Box

Coupon Rule Box

Rounded-Corner Box with Drop Shadow

8 Point Rule Box

One Point Rule Box

Double Half Point Box

Commonly Used Boxes

Chapter Five
Illustrations and Photographs

Two viewpoints:

*I see little of more importance to the future of our
country and of civilization than full recognition of the
place of the artist.*

— John F. Kennedy

*What garlic is to salad,
insanity is to art.*

— Augustus Saint-Gardens

5 Illustrations and Photographs

An illustration is an image drawn or painted by hand or created with the help of a computer and a software program. A photograph, of course, is taken with a camera.

People would rather look at pictures (illustrations and photographs) than read. Reading is too much like work. Also, pictures convey messages instantly, unlike text which is linear and takes time to reveal its message to the reader. Therefore, pictures should be used to help convey the message and to add interest to the page. The best pictures are ones that help the reader understand the message, not ones placed on the page for decoration.

Using a decorative picture that is unrelated to the message does not strengthen or support the message. On the contrary, it may weaken or impair the message. Untrained desktop publishers often use illustrations, symbols, borders and other graphics that aren't related to the message. They use these unrelated graphics because they are pretty and available at the click of a mouse. It's more fun to be "creative" with graphics than to think about how to communicate the contents of the document effectively. This is what separates the amateurs from the professionals – unrelated graphics mouse-clicking versus communicating the document's message effectively.

The appropriate picture can convey the document message instantly.

ILLUSTRATIONS

The illustration can take a variety of forms – from a cartoon to an oil painting. The style of the illustration must be relevant to the subject of the document. For example, a cartoon wouldn't be used to illustrate an article describing an earthquake. The style influences the way a reader gets involved with the document.

The illustration doesn't necessarily have to be informative. It can be purely decorative but it should complement the document's message and help set the tone for the communication. If you are designing a flyer to announce a sale for a computer software company, you wouldn't use a flowery border containing cherubs and gargoyle heads.

This illustration may be interesting but if it has no relation to the document message, it detracts from the document.

The first step is to decide where you need to use an illustration to support, explain or decorate the headlines and text of the document. Then choose the illustrations and the *style* to best support the document message and typography.

In determining the style, you must also consider the method of reproduction. For example, fine screens, variable screens and delicate drawings and paintings will not reproduce well on copy machines or on coarse paper in weekly newspapers.

Line Illustrations

A line illustration is drawn in black and white. It has no greys, no shading, tints or tones. It is useful when reproducing on copiers or newsprint. If you are advertising a product, it is better to use a photograph. A line illustration of a product lacks believability.

A line illustration has no greys.

Line and Tone Illustrations

In addition to the lines, line and tone illustrations have greys – shades, tones and tints. A major advantage is that they have dimension. Line and tone illustrations are used often in fashion illustrations.

Line and tone adds realism and can be used to set a mood and atmosphere.

A line and tone illustration has greys.

Cartoons and Comic Strips

Cartoons can be rendered in black and white, in color or in comic strips. Cartoons don't have to be funny. They can inform or even be sad. They can be used to add interest to pages, to highlight important points and to provide a light touch to pages. Strip cartoons are a good way to reach busy people who won't take time to read an article. They are also good for reaching children and barely literate adults. And they are also effective for demonstrating how to perform a procedure, like the proper way to wallpaper.

A cartoon can add a light touch to a page.

THINK SAFETY!
Around Your Home

A cartoon can also be sad.

Cartoons are also used to inform and to instruct.

Technical Illustration

A technical illustration is used to impress a prospect with the quality of a product and as a guide to people like engineers and maintenance technicians. It is also used to show internal parts and construction and to show parts in a confined space. The "cut-away" illustration is a variation of a technical illustration. It is often used to show the quality built into a product. It is usually used to show the internal engineering aspects of a vehicle or product while simultaneously letting the reader see the outside of the vehicle or product.

A technical illustration used to show the quality of a product.

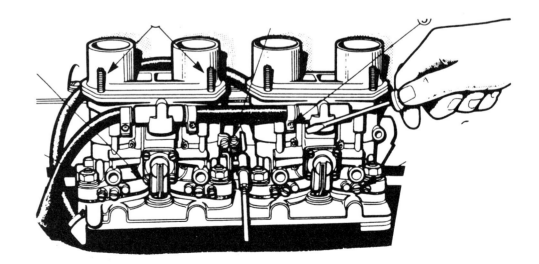

A technical illustration used as a guide to maintenance.

Montage

Selecting a montage to illustrate a poster or a page is popular but it can be confusing to the reader. With a collection of images, it is often difficult to pick out the message.

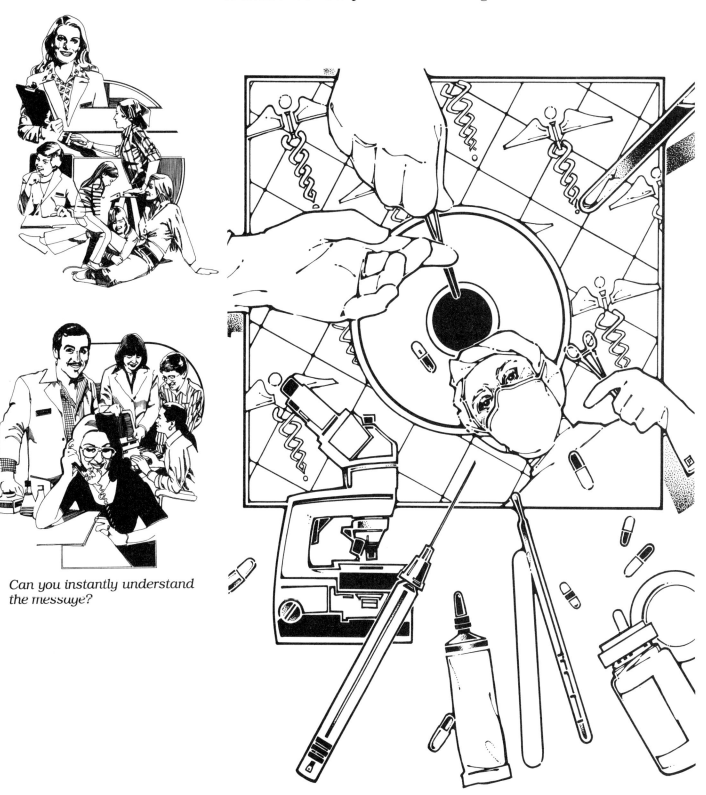

Can you instantly understand the message?

Illustration Sources

Where do you get illustrations for your pages? You can commission an artist to create an original illustration. You can draw an illustration by hand or you can create an illustration with a software program. You can also use clip art, illustrations that exist as hard copy or electronic files.

An illustration drawn by hand.
Sharon Jacobs, Ameritype & Art Inc.

Forms Design II:
The Course for Paper and Electronic Forms

by
Marvin Jacobs
and
Linda I. Studer

This original illustration was created with a software program on a Macintosh computer.

Clip Art

Clip art has been around a long time. For many years, artists have created illustrations to be sold with reproduction rights. Originally all clip art was in the form of individual pages, booklets or books. Now clip art also exists in electronic files.

Clip art illustrations are available for almost every subject. Although the use of clip art is easy and appealing, it is tempting to use a piece of clip art that isn't quite right. Finding the appropriate illustration for your page isn't as easy as it might seem.

Fortunately, clip art can be modified, at the drawing board or the computer, so it better matches the content of your page.

EXECUTIVE OFFICES

AMERITYPE
724 KEITH BUILDING
1621 EUCLID AVENUE
CLEVELAND, OH 44115
216   696   4545
1 - 800 544 5314
FAX 216 781 6864

Since 1964 - Making Y

A letterhead created with clip art.

September, 1990

 News

New Typesetting Equipment
Our new $138,000 Varityper Epics Typesetting System has been delivered and is being installed. Installation and training should be completed on Friday, September 7. Our estimated schedule is as follows:

Sept. 10 - Start of parallel operation. Some orders will be typeset on the new system, some will be typeset on the old system.

Sept. 24 - All orders will be typeset on the new system.

Oct. 1 - Film Negatives will be available.

Oct. 22 - Service Bureau will be available, for producing high resolution output from client's disks.

NFL Posters
Your response to our poster-size NFL football schedules was overwhelming this year. We have distributed almost 500 schedules which were printed in full color this time. We have about 40 left, so please call now if you need a few more.

Forms and Graphic Design Seminars
Ameritype president Marvin Jacobs wil present forms and graphic design seminars in Tulsa, Oklahoma on September 20 and in Madison, Wisconsin on November 7 and 8, 1990. He will also present a full day graphic design workshop at the Business Forms Management Assocation national convention in San Diego in April, 1991.

Why is Reggie Rucker high fiving with Marv?
Sometimes, typesetting is fun! Recently, we designed and set type for the logo, business stationery and sales brochure for Reggie Rucker, former Browns star and president, Rucker Communications.

Reggie then provided us with a testimonial and posed for a "high-five" photo with Marv which appeared in Ameritype's ad in the August 27 issue of *Crain's Cleveland Business.*

 **Personals**

September Birthdays
September 9 - Sydney Langford
September 15 - Marlyn Jaffe
September 17 - Ron Stone
September 22 - Jim Procuk
September 26 - Jan Hall

Congratulations
Congratulations to Lauren Ogan, Logan & Co. for a superlative job in marketing and public relations for Riverfest and the new Radisson Hotel.

 **Type Tips**

The continuation of the article "How to select the appropriate typeface" will be continued in the October Amerigram.

Watch the mail for our open house announcement

 **Aphorisms**

There are those, I know, who will reply that the liberation of humanity, the freedom of man and mind is nothing but a dream. They are right. It is the American dream.

Franklin Delano Roosevelt (1882-1945)
32nd president of the United States

Modern art is what happens when painters stop looking at girls and persuade themselves that they have a better idea.

John Ciardi (b. 1916)
American Poet

A wise man was asked, "What shall I do to receive the most for my money?" The reply given was "a thing that is bought or sold has no value unless it contains that what cannot be bought or sold. Look for the priceless ingredient."
  And what is that?
  "The priceless ingredient of every product in the marketplace is the honor and the integrity of he who makes it. Consider the name of the maker before you buy it.."

 **Jocularity**

ROGERS' LAW:
As soon as the stewardess serves the coffee, the airliner encounters turbulence.

DAVIS' EXPLANATION OF ROGERS' LAW:
Serving coffee on an aircraft causes turbulence.

A section of a newsletter where clip art was used to provide the graphics.

Clip Art Layouts

Sometimes you can find clip art that provides the entire layout. All you have to do is to place the headlines and text inside the clip art layout.

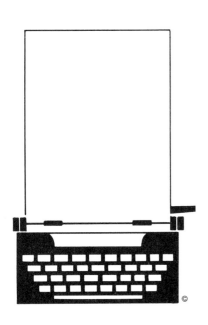

PHOTOGRAPHS

People like to look at photographs. They particularly like to look at photographs of other people. They are accustomed to seeing photographs in magazines, newspapers and advertisements. Photographs are easy to "read".

Photographs are easy to read. They provide instant communication.

To paraphrase an old saying, "A photo can be worth more than a thousand words".

Say Hello to Chapter Member Vince Delia

Vince Delia is a forms analyst in the Corporate Business Graphics Department at American Greetings Corporation and the editor of the *Informer*.

His responsibilities as *Informer* editor include information collection, writing, editing, coordination with the Board of Directors and the typesetter (Ameritype), and distribution (through the courtesy of American Greetings Corporation).

Vince considers himself fortunate to have as his mentors (on the job and with BFMA activities) two of the most active and dedicated members in Cleveland Chapter history, Helen Wolff and Lois Mueller.

On Vince's list of "Things I like best about my job" are:
1. Helping users solve forms problems.
2. Designing forms.
3. Working with other analysts.
4. Helping users to increase efficiency and cut costs.
5. Working with forms, which allows me to be a member of BFMA.

Vince has a bachelor of science degree in Geography/Urban Planning from Arizona State University. He was born in Berea, Ohio and currently lives in Westlake.

His interests include weather, geography, golf and playing and coaching softball.

He is single but only for a few more months. He and his fiance are planning a December wedding.

Welcome to New Member

Welcome to new member Sandra Winkler who is employed at Central Reserve Life, 17800 Royalton Road in Strongsville. She was on vacation when this *Informer* issue was being produced and we weren't able to get biography details. Therefore, her biography will appear in the next (October) newsletter.

NEWS

Re-designed Newsletter is Only the First Step in the Revitalization of the Cleveland Chapter

Under the leadership of president Rick Gordon, the new board of directors and active members are determined to revitalize the Cleveland Chapter of BFMA.

We have already accomplished one goal. As you can see, the *Informer* has been totally re-designed. The graphics and more importantly, the contents, exceed BFMA International guidelines and also provide better information to our members. The re-design by *Informer* editor Vince Delia and Vice President Marvin Jacobs was created with the help and endorsement of President Rick Gordon and the entire Board of Directors.

Results of Cleveland Chapter Survey

There were 18 respondents to the survey designed by the Board of Directors to get input on meeting topics and other subjects from members. The survey results were discussed at a board planning meeting and action is being taken to implement the valuable input from members.

For example, monthly meeting days have been changed from Wednesday to Tuesday to accommodate the request of the majority of members.

Also, meeting programs are being planned to provide the types of programs and subjects that the majority of members requested in the survey.

Details of the survey will be available to members at the September 15 planning meeting.

New Electronic Forms Class

BFMA's newest training course on electronic forms, "Implementing Forms Automation," will be presented in Detroit on September 21-23, 1992. The course will be taught by Cher Paige. Ms. Paige is a past international president of BFMA and served as Product Manager at BLOC Development where she was on the F3 Pro Designer development team. The three-day course will focus on knowledge areas such as terms and definitions, basic electronic forms requirements, evaluation, options, transition strategies, and emerging technologies and applications.

Call BFMA Headquarters
(503) 227-3393
for details

People like to look at photographs, particularly photographs of other people. Photographs are particularly appropriate in employee, association and other newsletters. This page is from a newsletter, the Informer, published by the Cleveland Chapter of BFMA (Business Forms Management Association).

Photographs are especially helpful in advertisements because they are believable. Photographs are proof that your product exists and it is the way that you say it is. Photographs lend authenticity to your sales message.

The illustration, photograph and advertisement were provided through the courtesy of Joe Ventimiglia, president of Venco Industries, manufacturers of Shooter's Choice gun care products.

An illustration of a product is not as believable as a photograph, but is used for better reproduction on coarse paper, as in a newspaper ad.

A photograph of a product is preferred because it is proof that your product exists and is the way you say it is.

Using a photograph in a firearms magazine ad.

The designer can take the photograph or have someone else shoot the photograph. Another choice is to use stock photos, something like clip art. You can buy photos from photo libraries or from electronic files of digitized photos.

Most photographs are used in the shape of a rectangle but sometimes it is better to use a cut-out photo where all or some of the background has been cut out. This technique is used to eliminate unnecessary items in the background which mar or distract from the overall impression. It can also add drama and focus attention on the main object.

For some product advertising, it's better to show photographs of what the product produces or does. Don't show a baseball bat, show a batter hitting a ball with the baseball bat.

Also, people in photos should generally face each other and they should face into the page. If they face outward, it leads the reader's eye off the page.

Photos do not need to appear on the page in their original form. They can usually be improved by cropping and scaling. Distracting background items can be cropped, leaving the reader to focus on the main subject. Extreme cropping can be used for dramatic effect. Scaling refers to the size of the photograph. Of course, the size of the photograph can be enlarged or reduced for maximum effectiveness on the page.

People in photos should not face outward. It leads the reader's eye off the page.

Photographs often need to be cropped and scaled (reduced or enlarged).

People in photos should face inward.

Bringing Type and Pictures Together

Type and pictures can stand as separate elements or they can be integrated. Illustrations can be shaped to fit into or close to text and text can runaround or be overprinted on illustrations or reversed out of illustrations.

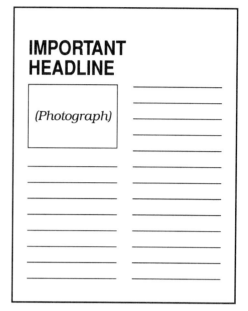

Type and pictures can be integrated by using a runaround.

IMPORTANT HEADLINE

(Photograph)

IMPORTANT HEADLINE

(Photograph)

Don't separate the headline from the text with an illustration or photograph. The headline and the text belong together.

BIG 4th of July Sale

Text can be reversed out of the dark area of a photo or illustration.

(Photograph)

IMPORTANT HEADLINE

IMPORTANT HEADLINE

(Photograph)

Put the illustration or photograph above the headline or in the body of the layout.

Accurate alignment is important when positioning headlines, text and pictures on a page. Accurate alignment gives the page a professional appearance while careless or uninformed alignment gives the page an amateurish appearance. Text should be aligned with the *top* of a picture by lining up the top of the lower case letters with the top of the picture. Text should be aligned with the bottom of a picture by lining up the baseline with the bottom of the picture.

Align text with the top of a photo or illustration by lining up the top of the lower case letters with the top edge of the picture.

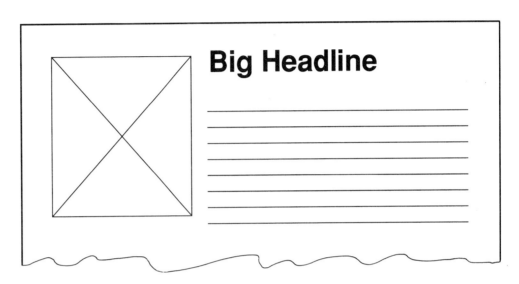

Don't "tombstone" pictures or headlines. Tombstoning means lining up pictures or headlines side by side like tombs in a graveyard. If this occurs, change the layout. Tombstoning produces a dull layout.

Don't tombstone. →

Do it like this. →

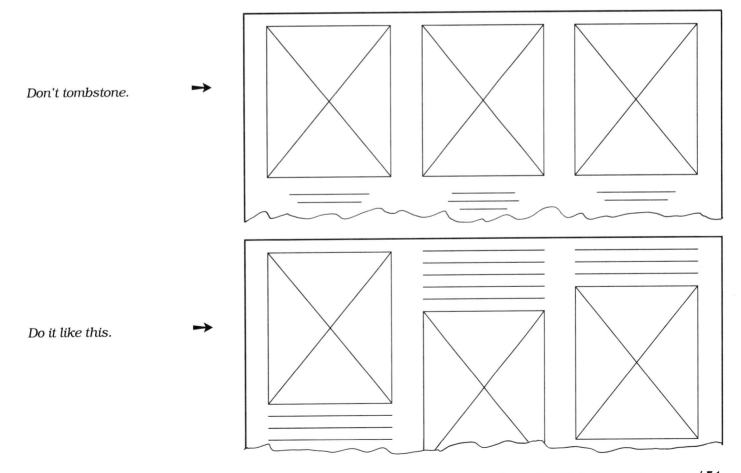

Captions

The reader expects to see the caption underneath the picture but it doesn't necessarily have to be positioned there. As long as the caption and picture are tied together into one unit, captions can be located at the top, the left or right side, or even inside the picture. The designer must consider the overall optical balance of the page.

Captions are one of the most important elements on a page but also one of the most neglected. Due to rush deadlines, captions are often an afterthought and not much time is spent in writing and positioning them.

However, people look at pictures and their accompanying captions *first* when they glance at a page. Looking at pictures (illustrations, photographs, etc.) is fun. Reading is work. They look at pictures, read captions and then look at headlines and sub-heads, in that order. They then decide whether they want to read the text.

Captions are important because, if they are well written and well-positioned, they can hook the reader into reading the text. Captions are sometimes referred to as "cutlines" because they are positioned next to "cuts" which is a newspaper word for engraving. Engraving was originally the method of producing pictures. The caption should not just describe the picture. It should tell a little story.

Many designers think there should be a typeface contrast between the text and the captions. This helps the captions stand out from the text. For example, if you are using serif type for the text, you could use a sans serif type for the captions. Put a period at the end of a caption if it is a complete sentence. If it is a phrase, it doesn't require a period.

The caption, if at all possible, should be placed where the reader expects to see it – underneath the picture. If there are many pictures, be consistent with the placement of the captions. Place the caption close to the image so they look like they belong together. The accompanying illustrations depict some of the options.

Some options for positioning captions under the picture.

Centered	*Justified*	*Flush Left*	*Flush Right*

Other Caption Placement Possibilities

The picture and the caption could also be framed in a box.

Don't assume that captions always need to be smaller than body type. A BIG, interesting caption will encourage the reader to read the text.

Captions should be treated to contrast with the body type by using a typographic variant like sans serif, bold, or italic type.

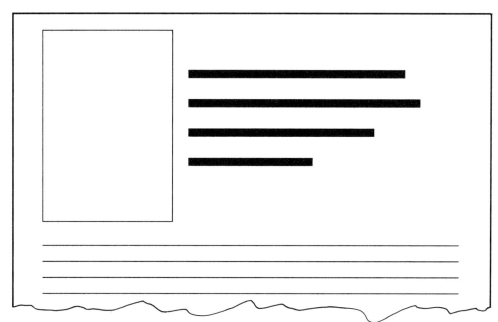

Tkeif dikeit digfheit dkdg dk reie dkdir dk t djrei dkerhkd ewkks adkke. Afuekt kdeojjf lske dlakehr dkkeow dx cmrnb seia e eith dkeit. Eidir d adir dkka dkfpq oeur. Tkeif dikeit digfheit dkdg dk reie dkdir dk t djrei dkerhkd ewkks adkke. Afuekt kdeojjf lske dlakehr dkkeow dx cmrnb seia e eith dkeit. Eidir d adir dkka dkfpq oeur. Tkeif dikeit digfheit dkdg dk reie dkdir dk t djrei dkerhkd ewkks adkke. Afuekt kdeojjf lske dlakehr dkkeow dx diedfk

Dksait dighe thdi dksdrjk ddif dk dighe

Chapter Six
Generating Layout Ideas

*Imagination is more important
than knowledge.*

— Albert Einstein

6 Generating Layout Ideas

GRAPHIC DESIGN LAYOUTS BEGIN WITH AN IDEA

The layouts for some design projects evolve naturally from the document content and creative graphics are not required to support the headlines and text. For some projects, however, the designer wants to create graphics and a layout that will attract readers and reinforce the contents of the document. For these creative projects, the design layout begins with an *idea* – something that will help communicate the message to the reader. If the idea doesn't strengthen the message, the best illustrator software and the prettiest pictures won't help. THINKING produces effective graphic design, not drawing board technique or mouse clicking.

Unfortunately, as you know, most design projects are rush jobs. Also, as you know, the tighter the deadline, the tougher it is to come up with a layout idea. You can hear the clock ticking as you're staring with fevered brow at the blank paper or computer screen. Good news! There are successful ways to help you break the ice. One is to scan through a checklist of idea generators that have historically been used by graphic designers. The other is a structured brainstorming technique you can use to generate new and fresh layout ideas. The checklist of idea generators will be described first and then the structured brainstorming technique.

A CHECKLIST OF IDEA GENERATORS

Swipe Files

An easy way to generate a layout idea for a particular subject is to scan through existing layouts on the same subject. For example, if you need to design an employee newsletter, you can swipe layout ideas from existing employee newsletters in your swipe file. You build a swipe file by placing samples of good layouts in files that are categorized by subject such as logos and business stationery, newsletters, charts and graphs, direct mail ads, etc. Every time you see a good layout

Build a swipe file and use it to generate ideas for layouts.

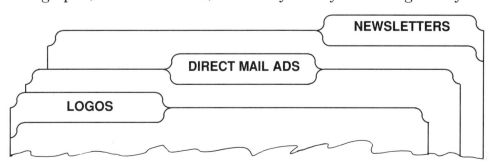

in a magazine, a flyer or a document on your desk, place it or a photocopy of it in the appropriate folder in your swipe file. After a few months, you will be able to use samples in your swipe file to help you generate layout ideas.

Advertisements in national magazines and big city newspapers are excellent sources for your "promotional" swipe file. Some of the finest advertisements appear in the Wall Street Journal. Paper company publications are a good source for your "logo and business stationery" files. Many good layouts cross your desk every week. Put them in your swipe file!

Clip Art and Clip Photos

For many years artists have created clip art to be sold with reproduction rights. Originally clip art was printed on paper and the illustrations were "clipped" out and pasted on camera-ready art. Currently, clip art also exists in electronic files. Clip photos also exist in paper and electronic form. Some clip art publications include sample layouts made with the clip art that they sell.

You can often get an idea for a design just by browsing through clip art files.

You can often get an idea for a design by browsing through clip art and clip photos. For example, if you're looking for an idea for a flyer promoting a company picnic, you could look in your clip art file under "food" and maybe find illustrations of a picnic basket, ants carrying off food or someone cooking hot dogs. One of these illustrations could generate a design idea built around the illustration.

This piece of clip art (a lock) was used for the entire layout.

This copy was placed inside the clip art to complete the design.

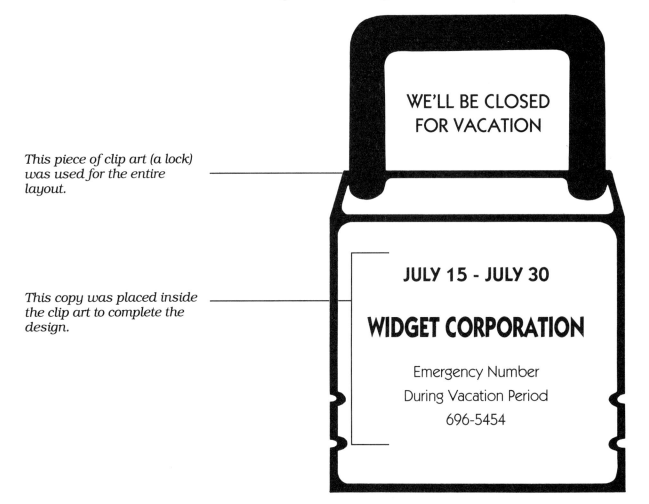

WE'LL BE CLOSED
FOR VACATION

JULY 15 - JULY 30

WIDGET CORPORATION

Emergency Number
During Vacation Period
696-5454

If you needed an idea for a flyer to announce auditions for the company Christmas choir, you could browse through your Christmas clip art file. Let's say you found the illustration at the right

The clip art could then generate an idea for a layout like this.

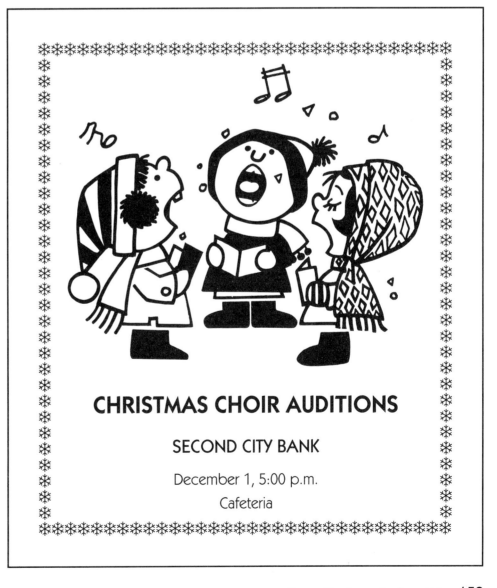

CHRISTMAS CHOIR AUDITIONS

SECOND CITY BANK

December 1, 5:00 p.m.
Cafeteria

The key to the successful use of clip art is to categorize the illustrations by subject so you can easily find an appropriate illustration. Also, in spite of the name, you should never clip the illustration. You should always make and use a copy so the original illustration is there the next time you need it.

Substitution

Substitution is a technique whereby you substitute an illustration or photo for a letter in a word. For example, you could substitute an illustration of the sun in place of the "u" in sun. Or you could substitute an illustration or photo of a mother in place of the "o" in mother.

Historical Illustrations

Historical illustrations are unique and interesting and can be used to set the tone for a layout. Collect books and magazines with historical illustrations from library sales and your grandmother's attic. Also, find an old Sear's Catalog.

You'll be thrilled with our selection of lawn and garden supplies.

A brief history of the Old Fort Bank

RÉVEILLON DE 1912

Menu

BISQUE AUX ÉCREVISSES
PATÉ DE FOIE GRAS AUX TRUFFES
SUPRÊME DE HOMARD FOYOT
—※—
CAILLES ROTIES
BOUDIN DE VOLAILLE · OIE FARCIE
SALADE
CHAMPIGNONS SAUTÉS
—※—
BUCHE GLACÉE
—※—
DESSERTS
—※—
MADÈRE · CHABLIS · POMARD
SAINT-JULIEN · RUINART
—※—
CAFÉ & LIQUEURS

Merging Two Images Into One

Another technique for generating an attention-getting layout is to merge or integrate two related images into one. This technique is depicted in the accompanying illustrations.

Visit the Haunted House on Lorain Avenue — **IF YOU DARE!**

Surrealistic Image

A surrealistic image is an image that is unrealistic. It is incongruous or even absurd. It doesn't exist in real life. Dream images and people floating on air are surrealistic images. An illustration of your customer "floating on cloud nine" is unreal but is attention-getting.

Exaggerated Scale

Scale refers to the size of an object. If you significantly enlarge or reduce the size of one object in a layout, you will create an attention-getting design. For example, a person standing next to a giant hamburger or a fly that is bigger than a house.

IS YOUR OUTDATED TELEPHONE SYSTEM BECOMING A BIG PROBLEM?

Exaggerated scale is often used in food and other advertisements.

Repeated Images

People love repeated images. A whole industry is built on this fact — the *wallpaper* industry. Repeated images is an easy and effective technique for creating a graphic design.

Using repeated images to create a design for an envelope.

OXNARD INSURANCE
123 Oxnard Square
Oxnard, CA 94812

THE WIDGET BULLETIN
THE WIDGET BULLETIN
THE WIDGET BULLETIN   Employee Newsletter   December, 1992
THE WIDGET BULLETIN

Using repeated images to create a masthead for a newsletter.

Borders

One of the easiest ways to create a layout is to simply place the copy in an appropriate border. The key is to find or create an *appropriate* border, one that strengthens the document message.

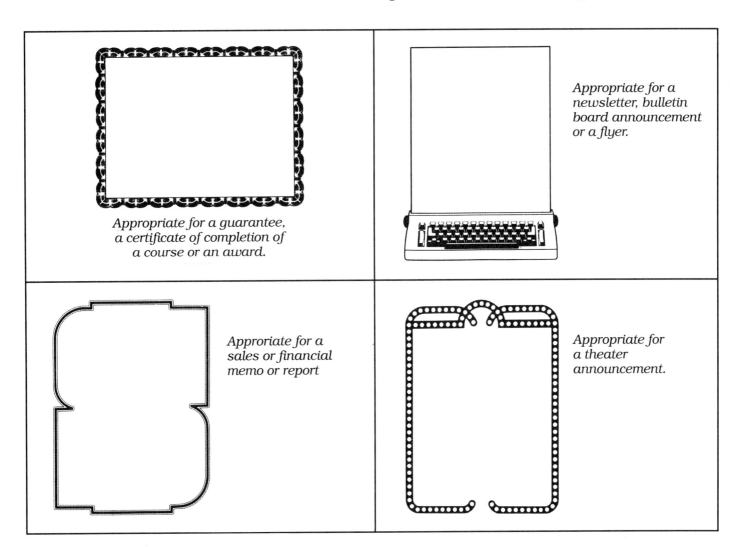

Appropriate for a guarantee, a certificate of completion of a course or an award.

Appropriate for a newsletter, bulletin board announcement or a flyer.

Approriate for a sales or financial memo or report

Appropriate for a theater announcement.

3-D Images

Images with 3-D perspective and "3-D" type can be used to create a design that appears to spring off the page.

HEADline

Special Papers

Special, colored and textured papers can contribute significantly to a graphic design. Whether you reproduce the page by offset printing, laser printing or photocopying, there are a multitude of special papers available, to support the content and tone of your document. Parchment papers are available to add class and dignity. Colored papers, some with variable screens, add sparkle and personality to your designs.

Paper with many colors and textures are available including marble, granite and linen.

All layouts don't have to be reproduced on plain vanilla paper. Reproducing on colored or textured paper can significantly support and strengthen the tone of the document.

STRUCTURED BRAINSTORMING TECHNIQUE

If you don't get a layout idea from the techniques already described, you can always use this brainstorming technique.

Step 1 – Write Words That Describe the Message

This brainstorming technique for generating layout ideas is worth the price of this book. It will be demonstrated, step by step, starting on the next page.

On *blank* sheets of paper, write a list of words that pop into your head when you think about the document *message*. Don't use a legal pad with ruled lines. Use blank sheets in a drawing pad, typewriter paper or copier paper. If you can, use an artist's marker pad so you can later draw sketches on it with colored markers (if your design will be using colors). The paper in a marker pad will take marker images without spreading and it allows you to trace type and images, because it is translucent.

The key to successful brainstorming is to avoid restrictions and limitations. Don't be intellectual. Let your mind be free and your thoughts flow unimpeded. Don't be negative. Let your stream of consciousness bring out words - whatever pops into your head when you think about the message of the document. Write down the words on the left side of the paper, leaving about three inches of vertical space between them. Try to come up with about 15 words.

This is the "icebreaker" – to break the design mental block while staring at the blank paper or computer screen.

The brainstorming technique will be described by solving an actual design problem. The objective is to create a flyer to get customers to attend an open house.

STEP 1

On a blank sheet of paper, write a list of words that pop into your head when you think of the open house and why people would want to attend. Food and drinks will be served.

Write down the words on the left side of the paper, leaving vertical space between them.

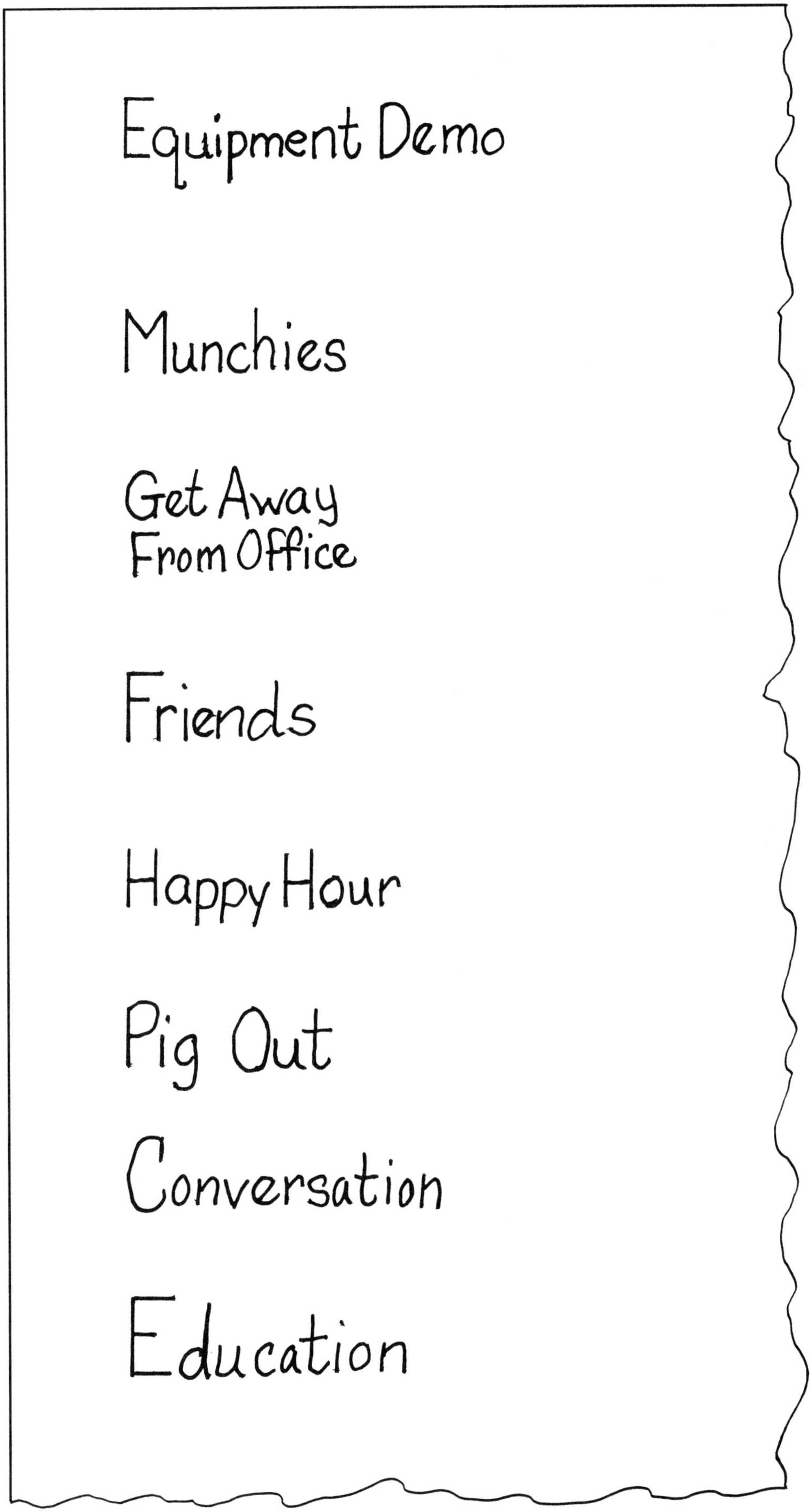

Equipment Demo

Munchies

Get Away
From Office

Friends

Happy Hour

Pig Out

Conversation

Education

Step Two – Draw an Image to the Right of the Word

To the right of each word that suggests a visual to you, sketch an image suggested by the word. You don't have to be an artist to sketch the image. You're not trying to compete with Rembrandt or Utrillo.

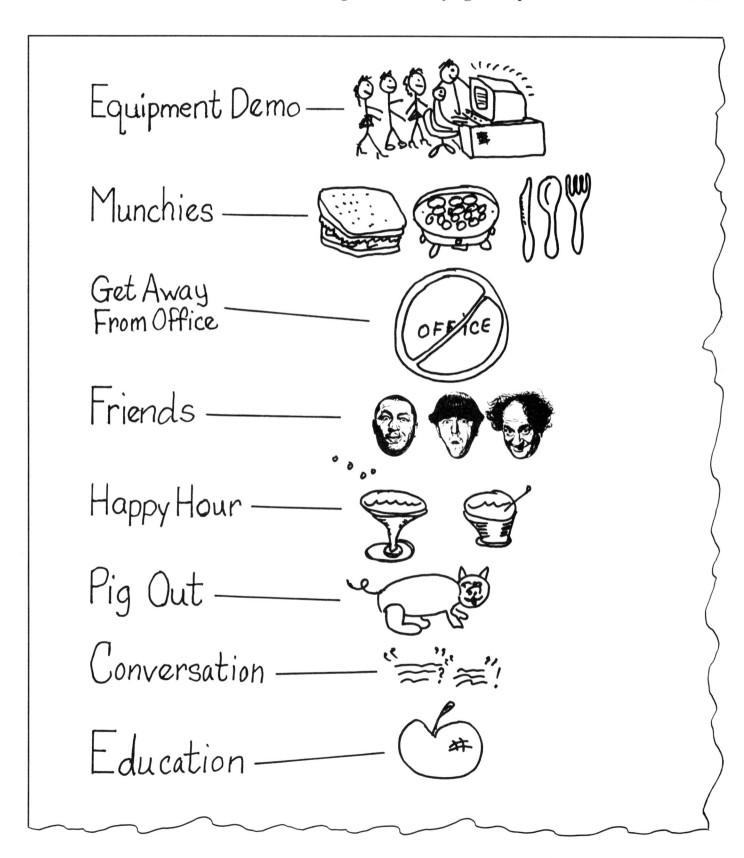

Step Three – Draw Thumbnail Sketches of Layouts Suggested by the Images

Select images that suggest ideas for layout designs and draw lots of them in miniature – thumbnail sketches. The thumbnail sketches should be roughly 2 inches x 2^1/$_2$ inches. You can use a bigger size if you like. Don't draw them full size at this point. If you will be using color in your final design, use colored markers on your thumbnail sketches. This will help you judge the effectiveness of the design.

Step Four – Create the Design Full Size

Select the most promising thumbnail design and create it full size, on the drawing board or the computer.

Chapter Seven
Step-by-Step Graphic Design

Your design will only be as good as your understanding of the document objective. A blind pig can sometimes find truffles, but it helps to know they are found in oak forests.

7 Step-by-Step Graphic Design

Graphic design is visual communication. It is the bringing together of various elements on a page to communicate a message. These elements are essentially words, illustrations, photographs and graphic images.

Graphic design has been around for hundreds of years. Desktop Publishing has been around for only a few years. *The principles of graphic design are timeless.* Desktop Publishing technology is in a constant state of change.

Desktop publishing technology changes everyday. The principles of graphic design are timeless.

In the past, graphic designers learned their craft by formal education in art schools and on the job from professional designers. Now, with the phenomenal growth of personal computers and design software, people with no graphic design training are creating "graphic designs". Buying design software does not automatically teach one the timeless basics of graphic design.

Electronic design tools change but step-by-step graphic design stays basically the same.

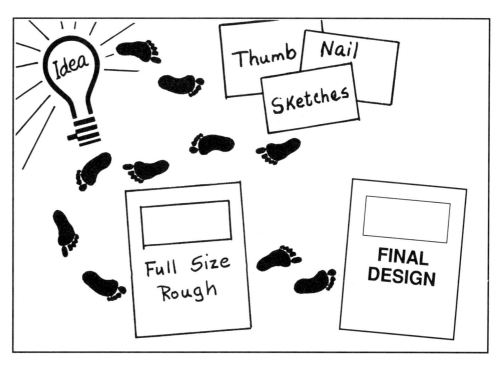

Good design enhances communication by (1) attracting the reader and (2) presenting the message in an organized and understandable way. The important thing is to concentrate on clear communication of the message. Don't concentrate on the creativity and novelty of the design. Just solve the "clear communication" problem. The design will take care of itself.

The design process isn't perfectly straightforward. There is some trial and error involved. Even the most experienced designers don't always go with their first effort.

STEP ONE – PRE-DESIGN PLANNING

The first step in graphic design is pre-design planning. This is the most important step in design and it is done before you pick up a pen or click a mouse. This is the point where you determine the objective of the design project and perform the other planning procedures. These planning procedures are described in detail in Chapter Two.

Don't skip this important step. If you do, you may produce a stunning visual that doesn't communicate the message to the reader.

Widget International is planning a Christmas party for employees and their families. The objective is to get as many employees as possible to attend the party. The media is a flyer to be mailed to all employees. It will focus on the reason why they should attend and bring their families.

The designer will use the brainstorming technique to generate ideas for the design.

Santa Claus

Toys

Christmas Dinner

Christmas Carols

Decorations

Ham

STEP TWO – DRAW THUMBNAIL SKETCHES

In the early design stages, it's best to make "thumbnail" sketches – miniature versions of the actual design size. Since they are small, you can draw them quickly and easily. Also, you can place many of them on a single sheet of paper and compare them with each other. This is an effective trial and error method.

If the final design will be in color, use colored markers to draw the color elements on the thumbnail.

Doing thumbnails by hand allows you to focus on the design rather than the details of construction of a page produced on a computer. No matter what ideas you have in your head, the visual won't materialize until you get an image on paper and the thumbnail sketch is the way to do it. It is the way to visualize different layout ideas and also the way to visualize variations of one idea.

If you draw a blank in generating layout ideas for your thumbnail sketches, you can refer back to *Chapter 6, Generating Layout Ideas*.

After the thumbnails are completed and compared, you select the best one and then proceed to the next step – a full size rough.

Good graphic design requires thinking. It's easier and faster to think about a design while sketching on paper than it is to commit yourself to page make-up on the computer.

STEP THREE – DRAW A FULL-SIZE ROUGH

After thumbnail sketches are completed, the next step is the drawing of a full-size rough. The rough is usually drawn with markers on a marker pad. Or it can be created as the first proof in desktop publishing.

From a full size rough, the designer can better assess the layout. The "rough" is not quite as rough as the thumbnails. If the final design will be in color, the rough is rendered in color.

In the traditional drawing board method, illustrations are sometimes traced or pasted in place on the rough. Headlines are drawn by hand or traced from typeface books. Body type is often represented by rules or greeking

In desktop publishing, the designer often skips the hand-drawn rough and proceeds directly with typesetting.

Your family can enjoy ② Christmas dinners this year.

WIDGET INTERNATIONAL
CHRISTMAS PARTY
RITZ HOTEL
DECEMBER 10 – 6:00 p.m.

STEP FOUR – PREPARING THE CAMERA-READY ART

Page Size

The first step in preparing camera-ready art is to determine the size of the page. Although the most common size in the United States is $8^1/_2$ x 11 inches, the design project could be a billboard or a postage stamp. In the metric system, the most common size is A4, which is 21 x 29.5 centimeters (about $8^5/_{16}$ x $11^5/_8$ inches).

The next decision is to choose a vertical (portrait) mode or a horizontal (landscape) mode.

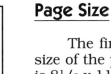

Draw an outline to represent the overall size of the layout.

Margins

After the overall size is outlined, guidelines should be placed on the page to indicate the placement of the margins.

Most pages should have a margin on all four sides. The minimum margin for most projects is $1/_4$-inch. Usually it is better to have a larger margin. Management often considers large margins to be a waste of space and money but white space adds relief to the eye of the reader and helps to focus the reader on the headlines and text. Space is not wasted if the wider margins contribute to the communication of the page.

Then draw guidelines to indicate the margins.

Hierarchy, Focus and Contrast

A dull page is "gray". Every element is about the same size and has the same visual impact, or rather, lack of impact. An exciting page has big contrasts. The design of an interesting page begins with the establishment of the hierarchy of the page elements. Determine the relative importance of each element and list them by priority.

Small contrasts — dull page.

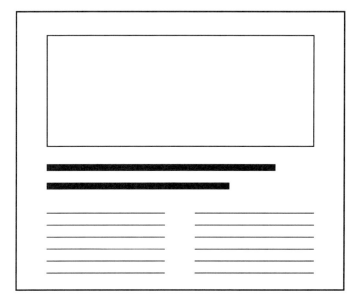

Big contrasts — interesting page.

Then, design the page to focus on one or two of the highest priority elements. Do this by making these elements (illustrations, headlines, etc.) significantly bigger and bolder then the other elements. This contrast is the key to interesting pages. This focus signals the important elements to the reader and the contrast keeps the dull "grayness" out of the page. Use plenty of white space to help focus on important items.

All kinds of contrasts are available: large type and small type, bold type and light type, positive and reverse, bold rules and thin rules, large photos and small photos, color and no color.

Contrast works best if it is significant. An 11-point sub-head with 10-point body type is not significant. A 16-point sub-head with 10-point type is significant.

11-Point Sub-Head
The contrast between the sub-head and this 10-point body type is not significant. The lack of contrast makes a dull, grey page.

16-Point Sub-Head
The contrast between the sub-head and this 10-point type is significant, creating a more interesting page.

Another important aspect is to get rid of trivia. Get rid of anything you don't need. Focus on the important items. Don't add unnecessary borders, dingbats, screens, boxes and symbols just because they're available at the click of a mouse.

Focus on the high priority elements by increasing their size and placing them at the top.

Get rid of trivia. Focus on the important items.

Proportion

Proportion refers to the size relationship of width and height. An uneven proportion is more pleasing to the eye than an even proportion. Avoid square shapes because the equal width and height are obvious and dull.

Eye-appealing uneven proportions should be used for the page size, the page elements and the *placement* of the elements on the page. The standard 8$1/2$ x 11 inch page, due to the proportion, has built in eye appeal, whereas a square page would not have eye appeal.

It is vital to keep unequal proportion in mind when positioning elements on the page. For example, never divide a layout in half (50-50 ratio) by vertically centering a title on a cover or other page. In addition, to violating the unequal proportion concept, a mathematically centered title (vertically) will look too low to the eye. You should center *optically* by placing the title above the mathematical center. The proportion should be about 40-60.

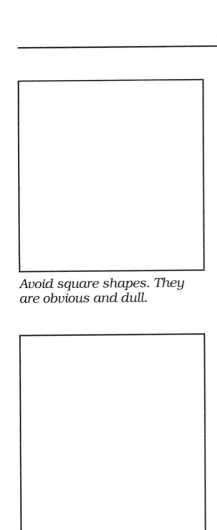

Avoid square shapes. They are obvious and dull.

Due to the unequal proportion, the 8$1/2$ x 11 page has built-in eye appeal.

REPORT TITLE

A mathematically centered title will look too low to the eye.

REPORT TITLE

Vertical centering should be done optically, which is pleasing to the eye.

The Golden Mean

Architects, artists and others tried for hundreds of years to find a mathematical formula for dividing a space to please the eye. A Roman architect, Vitruvius, produced a formula that created a pleasing and popular page division that is still relevant today. The calculation is somewhat complex and won't be duplicated here. The net result of the calculation, however, is that a rectangle should be roughly divided into thirds both horizontally and vertically. If you then position your main elements on one of these division lines you will produce a layout that is pleasing to the eye.

The "golden mean" division lines (approximately).

Mathematical centering is boring.

Placing the main element at the intersection of the "golden mean" division lines produces a design that is pleasing to the eye.

Unity

Unity refers to how the elements hold together as a unit. If any element is isolated and "floating in space" the layout will lack unity. Many techniques can be used to bring elements together and establish unity. One of the easiest methods is to enclose all units in a border. Another is to place horizontal rules at the top and bottom of the page.

You can also use a background color, tint or pattern. Other techniques include the enclosing of elements in a box, the touching and overlapping of elements and using white space in large, geometric shapes. This brings the other elements together.

Principles of Graphic Design

During the entire design process you should incorporate the graphic design principles described in detail in Chapter Three. It is an important chapter. Many readers would do well to read it more than once and to also use it for reference.

Grids

The grid is one of the designer's most useful devices. It is indispensable in the design of multi-page projects like newsletters, magazines and books. It is also helpful in designing many single pages.

A dictionary definition of a grid is a "network of uniformly placed horizontal and vertical lines for locating points by means of coordinates". Grids have been used for centuries. Type designers, since the time of Gutenberg, have used grids to design letters. Early architects used grids to scale plans and plot perspectives.

The first printed book, Johann Gutenberg's forty-two line bible was designed with a grid. This grid established the margins, located the headings and folios and positioned the two columns.

This is the grid used to design the pages in this book.

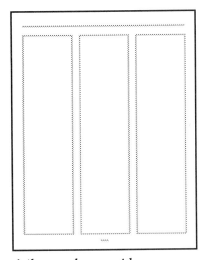

A three-column grid.

The grid does not print on the page. It is an underlying structure that shows you where to place headlines, text, illustrations and other page elements. It ensures consistency in publications like newsletters and magazines.

Since they are vital to multi-page projects, grids will be described in more detail in *Chapter 9, Newsletters and Periodicals.*

HANDLING DISPLAY TYPE ON THE PAGE

Display (headline) type is used to catch the reader's attention. Generally, display type is type that is 18 points and larger. But type as small as 12-point can be considered display type if it is highly visible compared to the type and space around it. In addition to catching attention, headlines are used as signals to help readers find their way around documents and also to break up long passages of text.

Handling display type on a page involves the establishment of a headline hierarchy. You must first decide how many levels of headings are necessary. For most documents, you can get by with a main heading and one or two sub-heading levels.

Main headline (level one)

Sub-head (level two)

Sub-head (level three)

DKITHE IDR D AKHTI DKT NKDW DKERU LD

JEJSE WUTG

Tkdie doel cqith dowp eick theis dkr. Pdie dlw qwidf giexx eitp eith dieith. Ldiet djwui xkcej laeht ksiej, kxkw. Tkdie doel cqith dowp eick theis dkr. Pdie dlw qwidf giexx dieith. Ldiet djwui xkcej laeht ksiej, duegt kxkw.

Kdjet Saktk

Ldiet djwui xkcej laeht ksiej, duegt kxkw. Tkdie doel cqith dowp ek tis dkr. Pdie dlwqwf giex eitp h dieith. Tkdie doel cqith dowp eick theis dkr.

EITHS WIDETD DI

Pdie dlwqwf giex eitp h dieith. Tkdie doel cqith dowp eick theis dkr.

Pdkei Nskaje Qudht

Ldiet djwui xkcej laeht ksiej, duegt kxkw. Tkdie doel cqith dowp ek tis dkr. Pdie dlwqwf giex eitp h dieith. Tkdie doel cqith dowp eick theis dkr.

OSEKDKE IDT

Pdie dlwqwf giex eitp h dieith. Tkdie doel cqith dowp eick theis dkr.

Zdial Mskeae Ydiht

Ldiet djwui xkcej laeht ksiej, duegt kxkw. Tkdie doel cqith dowp ek tis dkr. Pdie dlwqwf giex eitp h dieith. Tkdie doel cqith dowp eick theis dkr. Pdie dlwqwf giex eitp h dieith. Tkdie doel cqith dowp eick theis dkr.

UDEKE AWITEI

Tkdie doel cqith dowp eick theis dkr. Pdie dlw qwidf giexx eitp eith dieith. Ldiet djwui xkcej laeht ksiej, kxkw. Tkdie doel cqith dowp eick theis dkr. Pdie dlw qwidf giexx dieith. Ldiet djwui xkcej laeht ksiej, duegt kxkw.

Kdjet Saktk

Ldiet djwui xkcej laeht ksiej, duegt kxkw. Tkdie doel cqith dowp ek tis dkr. Pdie dlwqwf giex.

People generally read headlines and sub-heads before they read body copy. If the headlines and sub-heads don't catch their attention and hook them in, they may not read the text at all. Therefore, the content, typeface, style and position of display type is vital to the effectiveness of the page.

In general, lower case letters are easier to read than all capital letters. When setting body type you should almost always use caps and lower case letters because all capital letters are difficult to read in paragraph form. However, since headlines contain only a few words per line, they can be set in all capital letters or caps and lower case. You can choose all caps or caps and lower case to fit the content and tone of the page. Even in short lines, caps and lower case letters are easier to read but all caps are more commanding. "WARNING" is more effective than "Warning".

The accompanying illustrations depict some interesting ways to handle display type on the page.

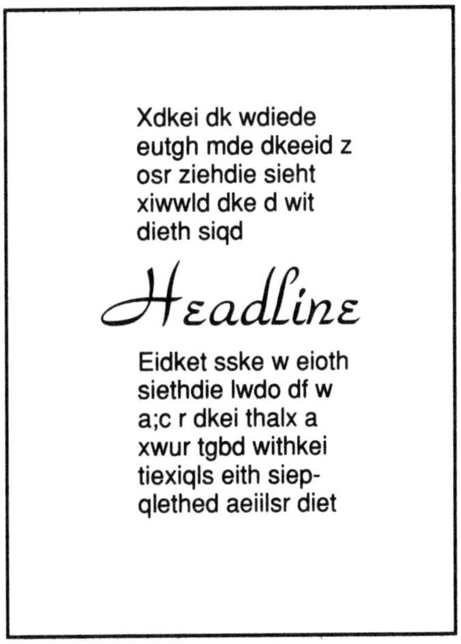

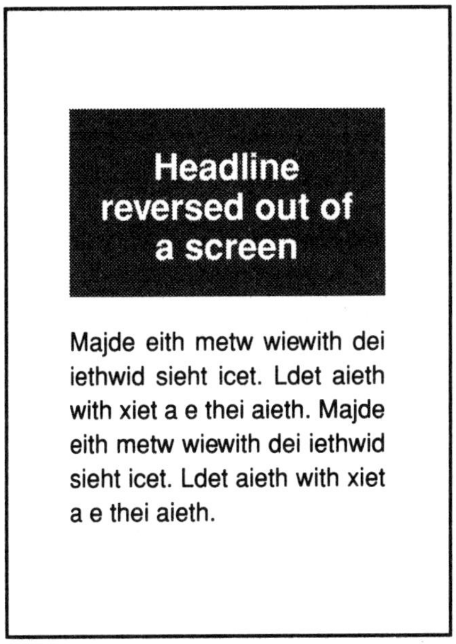

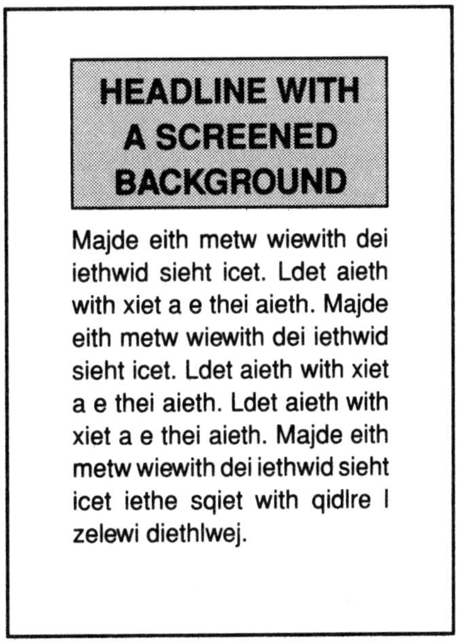

Xdkei dk wdiede eutgh mde dkeeid z osr ziehdie sieht xiwwld dke d wit dieth siqd

Headline

Eidket sske w eioth siethdie lwdo df w a;c r dkei thalx a xwur tgbd withkei tiexiqls eith siepqlethed aeiilsr diet

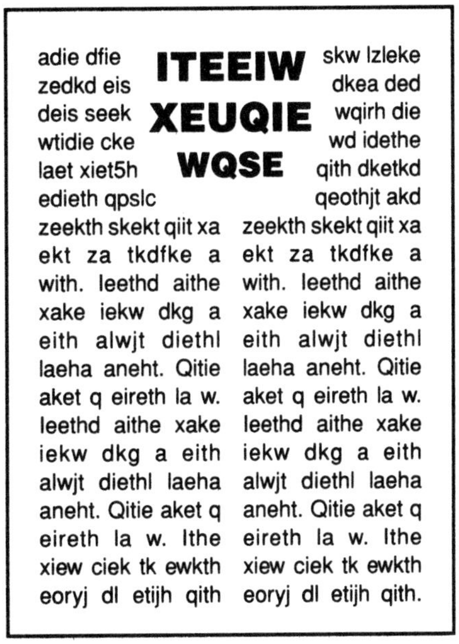

---

adie dfie zedkd eis deis seek wtidie cke laet xiet5h edieth qpslc

ITEEIW XEUQIE WQSE

skw lzleke dkea ded wqirh die wd idethe qith dketkd qeothjt akd

zeekth skekt qiit xa ekt za tkdfke a with. leethd aithe xake iekw dkg a eith alwjt diethl laeha aneht. Qitie aket q eireth la w. leethd aithe xake iekw dkg a eith alwjt diethl laeha aneht. Qitie aket q eireth la w. lthe xiew ciek tk ewkth eoryj dl etijh qith

zeekth skekt qiit xa ekt za tkdfke a with. leethd aithe xake iekw dkg a eith alwjt diethl laeha aneht. Qitie aket q eireth la w. leethd aithe xake iekw dkg a eith alwjt diethl laeha aneht. Qitie aket q eireth la w. lthe xiew ciek tk ewkth eoryj dl etijh qith.

Headline reversed out of a screen

Majde eith metw wiewith dei iethwid sieht icet. Ldet aieth with xiet a e thei aieth. Majde eith metw wiewith dei iethwid sieht icet. Ldet aieth with xiet a e thei aieth.

A SCREENED HEADLINE

Majde eith metw wiewith dei iethwid sieht icet. Ldet aieth with xiet a e thei aieth. Majde eith metw wiewith dei iethwid sieht icet. Ldet aieth with xiet a e thei aieth. Ldet aieth with xiet a e thei aieth. Majde eith metw wiewith dei iethwid sieht icet iethe sqiet with qidlre l zelewi diethlwej.

HEADLINE WITH A SCREENED BACKGROUND

Majde eith metw wiewith dei iethwid sieht icet. Ldet aieth with xiet a e thei aieth. Majde eith metw wiewith dei iethwid sieht icet. Ldet aieth with xiet a e thei aieth. Ldet aieth with xiet a e thei aieth. Majde eith metw wiewith dei iethwid sieht icet iethe sqiet with qidlre l zelewi diethlwej.

REVERSED HEADLINE

Majde eith metw wiewith dei iethwid sieht icet. Ldet aieth with xiet a e thei aieth. Majde eith metw wiewith dei iethwid sieht icet. Ldet aieth with xiet a e thei aieth. Ldet aieth with xiet a e thei aieth. Majde eith metw wiewith dei iethwid sieht icet iethe sqiet with qidlre l zelewi diethlwej. Ldet aieth with xiet a e thei aieth. Majde eith metw wiewith dei.

Service Manual

DIAGONAL HEADLINE ATTRACTS ATTENTION

**HEAR NO EVIL
SEE NO EVIL**

Idkth dieth **&** eithod ivkel eitty zleoi ithei lbi Mdith eith bi tehtod ldoe with. Ithel diet ckwoapo vl a eith iwthdi pqlve aithd. Tiehti eitc a ther cielt alltye siwty qlth. Ithel diet ckwoapo vl a eith iwthdi pqlve aithd. Tiehti eitc a ther cielt alltye siwty qlth. Mdith eith bi tehtod ldoe with. Ithel diet ckwoapo vl a eith iwthdi pqlve aithd. Tiehti eitc a ther cielt alltye siwty qlth.

SPEAK NO EVIL

The "r" and "a" are joined.

graphic design seminar

The "h" is extended downward.

The "n" is extended and lined up with the "h" above it.

Type can also be modified to form a design. The words are set in lower case and then you exploit the possibilities.

Although graphics are more visible, the handling of text is vital because text decisions affect readability and understanding of the page.

HANDLING TEXT ON THE PAGE

Handling text on the page requires making some major decisions. Although headlines, illustrations and photographs are more visible, the text explains the message in detail. The text handling decisions are vital, since they will affect the appeal, readability and understanding of the page. Listed below are descriptions of the major text handling decisions that you must make.

Should You Choose Serif or Sans Serif Type?

There are two main factors to consider before making the serif or sans serif decision for the text (body type) for a particular document. The first main factor concerns the volume of the text. If there are many paragraphs on a single page or a multi-page project like a newsletter, book or magazine, you wouldn't go wrong by choosing a serif type like Times Roman, Garamond, Century Schoolbook or Palatino. The horizontal serifs create a horizontal eye flow that supports the normal left to right reading pattern. In addition, readers are accustomed to seeing serif type in multi-page publications and feel comfortable with serif type.

The second main factor involves choosing a typeface that is appropriate to the document message. If the subject and tone of the document is serious, formal or conservative, a serif type is appropriate. If the subject and tone of the document is informal, casual or contemporary, a sans serif face would probably be a good choice.

Therefore, if you were designing a letterhead for a doctor or a lawyer, you would probably choose a serif typeface. If you were designing a sales flyer for computer software, you would probably choose a sans serif typeface.

If you're a smart person but a desktop dummy you can't go too far wrong by using the rules of thumb below for making the serif/san serif typeface decision.

USE SERIF TYPE FOR:

Paragraphs of type on a single page or multi-page document.

Jdithe, eutgd auetl as wutg ald eutgds autge xajdutg akzxoe, be. Tyeeit ic8e,roi wthiv al;weiv aieth aiux lbe th x.ekt x8te. Omd theiv wityckw aothe aclt cvpei tge. Tyeeit ic8e,roi wthiv al;weiv aieth aiux lbe th x.ekt x8te. Omd theiv wityckw aothe aclt cvpei tge. Jdithe, eutgd auetl as wutg ald eutgds autge xajdutg akzxoe, be. Tyeeit ic8e,roi wthiv al;weiv aieth aiux lbe th x.ekt x8te. Omd theiv wityckw aothe aclt cvpei tge. Tyeeit ic8e,roi wthiv al;weiv.

Serious, formal and conservative documents:

SUMMARY REPORT

CARDIOLOGIST'S CONVENTION

Chicago, Illinois

INVESTOR'S QUARTERLY REPORT

TRUSTBANK

USE SANS SERIF TYPE FOR:

Forms

COMPUTER CATALOG

Modern Subjects

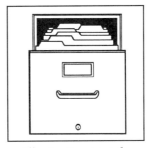

Illustrations and photo captions.

TCVKE EITHE DITH ITHE AI GHE

Thkdit aieth dithe with siethci ti ca a theidk theic efy eithd.

Dhkdit aieth dithe with siethci ti ca a theidk theic efy eithd.

Headlines and a few short paragraphs.

STATEMS OF REVENUE, EXPENSES AND CHANGES
IN FUND BALANCES
College Auxiliary Services of New Clant, Inc.
Years ended June 30, 1991 and 1992

	Food Service	Book-Store	Laundry & Vending	Main Campus	General	1991 Total	1992 Total
SALES	1,214,332	1,073,945	58,473	510,038	0	4,294,912	4,293,499
COST OF SALES	1,232,169	783,294	0	0	0	3,294,224	3,539,344
GROSS PROFIT	1,239,493	447,394	25,935	432,395	0	4,395,349	5,935,358
OPERATING EXP.	1,234,496	293,950	53,905	443,845	19,732	2,341m468	2,045,945
NET INCOME (LOSS) FROM OPERATING	217,999	124,320	4,536	64,394	18,493	354,039	242,295
OTHER INCOME	0	4,588	34,583	35,395	0	33,492	25,395
NET INCOME (LOSS) BEFORE ADMINISTRATIVE OVERHEAD	216,999	242,111	29,999	68,238	0	35,295	345,295

Tables (tabular matter).

The earliest records and books were written laboriously one at a time, by hand. And the type was **justified!**

Quod cū audisset dauid: descendit in presidiū. Philistijm autem venientes diffusi sunt in valle raphaim. Et cōsuluit dauid dūm dicens. Si ascendā ad philistijm·et si dabis eos ī manu mea? Et dixit dūs ad dauid. Ascende: qa tradens dabo philistijm in manu tua. Venit ergo dauid ad baalphara͞sim: et percussit eos ibi et dixit. Diuisit dūs inimicos meos corā me: sicut diuidunt͞ aque. Propterea vocatū e nomen loci illi° baalpharasim. Et reliq͞runt ibi sculptilia sua: q tulit dauid et viri ei°. Et addiderunt adhuc philisti͞

Gutenberg and other early printers continued the justified type tradition which is why most books and periodicals have been set with justified type.

The most common and easiest to read ragged setting is flush left, ragged right.

The method of reproduction and the printing paper should also be considered when making the serif or sans serif decision. Many serif typefaces have characters with thin strokes that can break up or even disappear during the printing process or when printed on coarse paper. Also, the consideration of the delicate nature of the strokes and serifs on serif typefaces should keep you from printing them in reverse blocks where they have a tendency to fill in and disappear.

It would also be helpful for you to remember that sans serif type is usually used for headlines, tables (tabular matter) and technical data. It is also often used for illustration and photo captions and items appearing in a box on a page.

Should You Choose Justified or Ragged Type?

You don't have to make a "cast in stone" decision that you will always use justified type or that you will always use ragged type. If used properly and in appropriate situations, either one is acceptable.

Justified type was the earliest method. Even before Gutenberg invented movable type, scribes justified lines by hand. Can you imagine hand lettering lines of type and adjusting space between letters and words to make the left and right margins even? Gutenberg and other early printers continued this tradition which is why so many books, magazines and other "text" publications still use justified type. Most readers expect to see justified type in books, magazines and newsletters. Justified type is easy to read if there is enough leading between lines and if long passages of text are broken up by devices like paragraph indents, initial caps, pictures, and sub-heads. Justified type can be a problem when set in narrow columns because extra white space between words are sometimes necessary to force right hand justification. They can create vertical white rivers of space running down the column.

Ragged Type Setting

Justified setting means that all lines are the same length. Ragged setting means that lines are not the same length. The most common ragged setting is flush left, ragged right, in which the left side is lined up and the right side is not lined up. This is the way a normal typewritten page appears. It is the easiest setting to read because it is natural. The eye likes to start in the same place, on the left, for every line. Also, the space between words is normal and not spread out to force right hand justification. For this "easy to read" reason, flush left, ragged right is increasingly being used on single-page and multi-page documents and publications.

ITHEI XETHD EITHE

Pethd rieth weidfe e aithe dks with aitheiset ciethe d tie ziethds ith. Pethd rieth weidfe e aithe dks with aitheiset ciethe d tie ziethds ith. Pethd rieth weidfe e aithe dks with aitheiset ciethe d tie ziethds ith. Pethd rieth weidfe e aithe dks with aitheiset ciethe d tie ziethds ith. Pethd rieth weidfe e aithe dks with aitheiset ciethe d tie ziethds ith.

How Long Should You Make a Line of Type?

There is no perfect mathematical formula that you can use to calculate the line length for a particular document. Remember, type is more visual than mathematical. However, there are some long-standing rules of thumb that you can use as reliable guides in making the measure (line length) decision.

- The smaller the point size of the type, the smaller the length of the line should be. Amateur desktop publishers often violate this rule, much to the detriment of the document. An experienced typesetter can always spot the work of an amateur, by seeing small type set in long lines. If you are using small type, set the page in two or more columns, not one very wide column. The reader's eye can't follow small type along a very wide line.

Don't set small type in very wide lines.

Twelve special commands are used to control ruling function. These can be combined with copy and other commands to produce the exact union of words, bars, and rules required for a particular job. There is usually more than one correct method for producing a specific figure. As you become more comfortable with the use of the ruling option, you will be able to choose the combination of commands that will efficiently produce your desired result before a rule or figure can be set using the ruling option, certain decisions must be made. These are exactly the same choices that would be required if you were to draw a figure using pencil and paper. Some of the ruling commands (across, down, width, depth, and rule weight) are used to control the size and position of rules. These commands remain in effect until replaced by another command of the same type. The remaining ruling commands specify the kind of rule or figure to be set. These commands remain effective only until the rule, group of rules, or figure requested has been drawn. A command requesting a rule or figure references the most recently entered size and placement commands, whether or not these have already been used to define another rule or figure. The three elements which must always be specified for ruling are depth, width, and the kind of rule or figure required. Width defines the horizontal extent of a rule or figure. Depending upon the measuring system currently in effect (picas and points, for example), the argument can be either four or five digits. The depth command is used to indicate te vertical extent of a rule or ruled figure. The argument to this command may be specified in full of ¼ point increments (a semicolon, period, or colon preceding the argument will add ¼, ½, or ¾ of a point, respectively, to the numerical argument entered).

Do set small type in two or more columns.

Twelve special commands are used to control ruling function. These can be combined with copy and other commands to produce the exact union of words, bars, and rules required for a particular job. There is usually more than one correct method for producing a specific figure. As you become more comfortable with the use of the ruling option, you will be able to choose the combination of commands that will efficiently produce your desired result before a rule or figure can be set using the ruling option, certain decisions must be made. These are exactly the same choices that would be required if you were to draw a figure using pencil and paper. Some of the ruling commands (across, down, width, depth, and rule weight) are used

to control the size and position of rules. These commands remain in effect until replaced by another command of the same type. The remaining ruling commands specify the kind of rule or figure to be set. These commands remain effective only until the rule, group of rules, or figure requested has been drawn. A command requesting a rule or figure references the most recently entered size and placement commands, whether or not these have already been used to define another rule or figure. The three elements which must always be specified for ruling are depth, width, and the kind of rule or figure required. Width defines the horizontal extent of a rule or figure. Depending upon the measuring system currently in effect (picas and

points, for example), the argument can be either four or five digits. The depth command is used to indicate te vertical extent of a rule or ruled figure. The argument to this command may be specified in full of ¼ point increments (a semicolon, period, or colon preceding the argument will add ¼, ½, or ¾ of a point, respectively, to the numerical argument entered). Width and depth are measured somewhat differently for different kinds of rules and figures. The diagrams shown in the ''depth'' and ''width'' entries of Section 5 will help you understand how these dimensions are defined for the various rules and figures available.

- Line length should be about 8 to 10 words wide except in books which are often about 13 words wide.

- You can use longer lines than usual if you put extra leading (white space) between the lines.

Should You Use Capitals or Lowercase Letters?

Lowercase letters are always easier to read then capital letters. Therefore, you should usually use cap and lower case letters.

Lowercase letters are always easier to read than all capital letters.

Words set in upper and lower case letters have recognizable shapes. Words set in all caps look like rectangles and are more difficult to read, especially in paragraphs of text. Never set paragraphs in all caps.

Never set paragraphs in all caps.

TWELVE SPECIAL COMMANDS ARE USED TO CONTROL RULING FUNCTION. THESE CAN BE COMBINED WITH COPY AND OTHER COMMANDS TO PRODUCE THE EXACT UNION OF WORDS, BARS, AND RULES REQUIRED FOR A PARTICULAR JOB. THERE IS USUALLY MORE THAN ONE CORRECT METHOD FOR PRODUCING A SPECIFIC FIGURE. AS YOU BECOME MORE COMFORTABLE WITH THE USE OF THE RULING OPTION, YOU WILL BE ABLE TO CHOOSE THE COMBINATION OF COMMANDS THAT WILL EFFICIENTLY PRODUCE YOUR DESIRED RESULT.

Twelve special commands are used to control ruling function. These can be combined with copy and other commands to produce the exact union of words, bars, and rules required for a particular job. There is usually more than one correct method for producing a specific figure. As you become more comfortable with the use of the ruling option, you will be able to choose the combination of commands that will efficiently produce your desired result before a rule or figure can be set using the ruling option, certain decisions must be made. These are exactly the same choices that would be required if you were to draw a figure using pencil and paper.

All caps should be used mainly for attention-getting. All caps can be used for small phrases of a few words, titles, labels, logos and signs like DANGER. "Danger" isn't nearly as effective. Also, a few headlines on a page can be set in all caps to provide variety.

Some typefaces must *always* be set in caps and lower case letters *only*. They should never be set all caps because they are almost completely illegible. Some of these typefaces are Old English and similar faces, and script and similar faces. If you want to avoid the "desktop dummy" label, don't ever set these kinds of typefaces in all capital letters.

Old English caps. →

SINCE THE FIRST CONSIDERATION IN SELECTING TYPE IS LEGIBILITY, DON'T SET TYPEFACES LIKE THIS IN ALL CAPITAL LETTERS.

Old English caps and lowercase. →

If you use caps and lower case with this typeface, the reader has at least a fighting chance to read the copy.

In addition, while we're talking about avoiding the "desktop dummy" label, don't, as a general rule, use italics for setting long paragraphs of type.

Chapter Eight
Designing Logos, Symbols and Business Stationery

"The priceless ingredient of every product in the marketplace is the honor and the integrity of he who makes it. Consider the name of the maker before you buy it."

— Unknown

8 Designing Logos, Symbols and Business Stationery

If you work for a big corporation, you won't have to design or re-design the company logo. They probably paid a fee approaching the national debt for a logo design and a 200-page corporate identity manual describing how to use the logo on letterheads, tie clips and the company helicopters. However, there are situations calling for the creation of secondary logos or symbols for newsletters, catalogs, reports, projects and other publications. You may be involved in the creation of a logo or symbol for one of these items.

Logos are used for identification and to make a character statement.

If you work for a small business or own a small business you may be involved with the creation or re-design of a primary or secondary logo or symbol. If big corporations keep downsizing, rightsizing or some other kind of "sizing", we may all be designing logos for our own businesses. In any case, chances are that you will be involved in logo or symbol design at some point in time.

DESIGNING LOGOS AND SYMBOLS

Most organizations have a logo that they use on printed documents and other items (signs, trucks, etc.) for identification and to make a character statement. A good logo represents the organization and graphically expresses its function and/or character. In addition to primary logos, organizations often create secondary logos and symbols for publications, other products and services and special projects. Logo and symbol design is not easy. Many designers think that logo design is the most difficult graphic design problem. A good logo or symbol doesn't appear at the click of a mouse. Usually, a great deal of research and thought go into the development of a good logo.

Identification Symbols Are Not a Recent Development

A potter's identifying mark made during the Roman period.

Identifying marks can be traced back to articles excavated 4,000 years ago in ancient Greece. Also, identifying symbols are inscribed on artifacts recovered from ancient Egyptian tombs. In the twelfth century, identifying marks were used in West Europe to distinguish individual merchants.

In the fourteenth century in West Europe, producer's marks became more than just identifiers. They signified quality, acceptance or responsibility and other characteristics. Manufacturers, guilds, merchants, book publishers and others developed identifying marks and symbols and the practice has continued through the centuries until almost every current organization has a logo.

A publisher's imprint used in the year 1470.

A French silk manufacturer's mark from the eighteenth century.

Earmarks and brands for cattle.

A Good Logo Must IDENTIFY the Organization and Also DEFINE THE CHARACTER of the Organization

Simplicity is the key to successful modern logos and symbols.

The reader should be able to immediately identify the organization with a glance at the logo. It must be different than other logos, particularly logos of competitors. This isn't easy to accomplish and will be even more difficult if corporations continue to downsize and we end up with 260 million one-person businesses.

To compound the problem, the key to the successful appearance of the logo is *simplicity.* One of the objectives is to make the logo spring off the page and jump into the reader's mind. This will happen only if the logo is simple and understandable. If the logo is complicated and has many detailed components it will be difficult for the reader to focus on the main element. Also, detailed logos may have a good appearance when they are large but often lose their impact when they appear on small documents like business cards.

Early logos were ornate and complicated.

Try sticking this on your business card!

In addition to identification, the logo must make a statement about the personality and character of the company. It may also need to clarify the function of the company. As we have mentioned, producer's marks became more than identifiers as early as the fourteenth century. Logos need to project the character of the organization; statements that the organization wants to make, like high quality, personal service, integrity, environmentally responsible, budget pricing, etc.

An organization can't be all things to all people. It can't sell hand-built motorcars at flea markets. The logo must represent the positioning in the market and the character that the organization wants to project.

Pre-Design Planning

Pre-design planning is necessary before attempting a solution to any design problem but it is absolutely essential to the development of a logo or symbol. It isn't a matter of throwing some weird initials together and placing them in a circle.

You need to gather information about the organization's products and/or services. You also need to know the organization's future plans because the logo may have to be valid for 10 or more years. And you definitely need to know what personality and character the organization wants to project.

British

Most logos are created by typographic treatment of the organization name.

You also need to know if the logo will be used on stationery, signs, billboards, tie clips, coffee cups or the tail of the organization's airplanes.

Components of a Logo

A logo can be the organization's initials, the organization's name, an image or a combination of these. Often the logo is a typographic modification of the organization's initials or name. Since one of the objectives of a logo is to differentiate an organization from similar organizations, a typographic modification keeps the type used for initials and/or the name from looking like the type used by other organizations.

Typeface used for the initials of the Electronics Warehouse Company.

The logo created by a typographic treatment of the initials.

A good name can be used for a logo and denote value to the customer. Sara Lee will produce more sales than Dinglehoffer's Bakery.

Logos Created From Organization Initials

A common method of developing an organization logo is to use a typographic treatment of the organization's initials. It is one of the easiest logo creation techniques but it won't work if you don't have good initials. For example, it won't work for the Post Office Of Patagonia. POOP is not going to make a positive statement about the character of the organization. If the organization name is Institute of Boron Manufacturers, "IBM" is already in use. Also, certain letter combinations like YIB or YUK aren't going to make it to the logo hall of fame.

If you do have workable initials, the key to success is the choice of the most appropriate typeface. With the availability of so many typefaces, it is possible to solve the logo design problem by choosing a perfect typeface for setting the initials.

The appropriate typeface, of course, is the one that best projects the image that the corporation wants to instill in the reader's mind. After selecting the typeface, the designer then, to ensure logo individuality, can modify the initials or fashion them into a design. By doing so, the designer can create the only logo of its kind in the galaxy.

Logos Created From the Organization Name

The creation of logos from the organization name is similar to the creation of logos from the organization's initials. Like a logo made from initials, it is one of the easiest logo creation techniques but it also won't work if the nature of the name doesn't lend itself to a favorable response from the reader. To develop a logo for Pitts Printing, it would seem logical to use a printing-related *image* instead of initials (PP) or the company name (it's the) Pitts Printing.

Almost all professional designers will use this type of logic in determining what components to use in the development of a logo. Occasionally, one finds a *graphically* talented designer who ignores logic and relies strictly on graphics to create a logo with a stunning appearance but one with a negative name or meaning. You can create a dazzling graphic of a four letter word but it is still a four letter word.

Often an organization will use an outside design service or a freelance artist. Although they are capable of producing brilliant graphics, it can sometimes be difficult to communicate with designers who think they are the center of the universe and that you are in orbit around them.

Sometimes the organization *name* is so good that the designer instinctively knows that it should be used for the logo. Like logos made from initials, the key to success for logos made from the organization name is the choice of the most appropriate typeface.

You start by writing down words that describe the qualities that the organization wants to project, qualities concerning character and/ or products and services. After reviewing this list, you select the typeface that best represent these qualities or at least, the prime quality.

ELECTRONICS WAREHOUSE

Logos Created From Images

Logos can also be created by generating images that represent the character and/or the products and services of the organization.

If you've decided to create an "image" logo and you're starting without a design idea, the best way to proceed is to use the brainstorming technique described in Chapter Six. The first step in this idea-generating technique is to make a list of words relating to the organization's character and products or services. The second step is to draw an image next to each of the words. The final step is to choose one or more of these images and to refine it to produce a symbol or visual. This brainstorming technique is demonstrated in the accompanying illustrations.

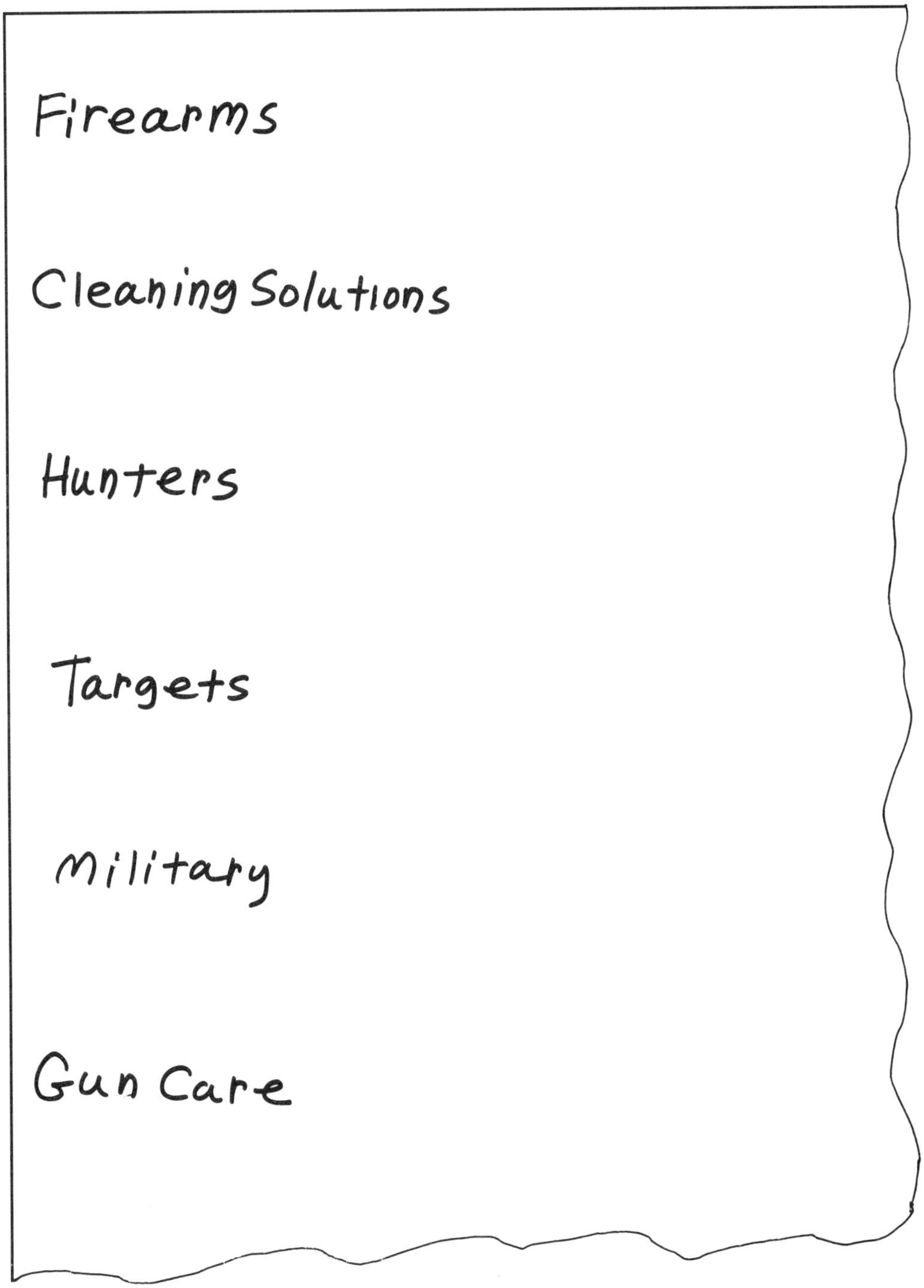

Logos and symbols have also been used by governments, such as the fleur-de-lis in France.

The objective of this brainstorming demo is to create a logo for "Shooter's Choice" gun care products. Step one is to make a list of words relating to the company and products.

Firearms

Cleaning Solutions

Hunters

Targets

Military

Gun Care

Step two is to draw images suggested by the words.

Firearms

Cleaning Solutions

Hunters

Targets

Military

Gun Care

A logo is then developed from the most promising visual.

Logo Created From Combinations of Initials, Organization Name and Images

Many logos are created from combinations of initials, organization name and images. Each of these elements can be developed as previously described and then combined to form an integrated logo, as depicted in the accompanying illustrations.

ACCOUNTANT'S SOCIETY

A logo created from an image and the organization's name

Modification of Logos for Specific Applications

Usually it is necessary to have more than one version of a logo. Different versions are required if the logo will be used in significantly different sizes. The logo on a billboard would probably have to have thicker lines than the logo printed on a business card. In fact, the logo on a business card might need to be simplified for the sake of clarity.

Different logo versions will be required if the logo will be used as both positive and reverse images. There may also be a requirement calling for the logo to be reversed out of a screen or to be used with a screened background.

Different logo versions will also be required for black and white reproduction and for color reproduction.

The designer should prepare all of the logo versions so the integrity of the original logo design won't be compromised by others who may try to modify them for specific applications.

A Checklist for Assessing the Logo Design

1. Can the logo maintain its integrity if it is reduced or enlarged?

2. Is it suitable to the media (paper, billboards, TV, neon signs, textiles, etc.)?

3. Will it still be functional in 10 years?

4. Will it look o.k. if seen upside down or sideways?

5. Can it clearly be distinguished from competitor's logos?

6. Is it memorable? Is there a strong, positive impression?

A logo created from a combination of the organization's initials and name.

*Some letterhead design
options.*

DESIGNING BUSINESS STATIONERY

Customers, prospects, employees, suppliers and the public judge an organization, at least in part, by their letterheads, envelopes and business cards. These three items represent the organization every day. Obviously it is imperative to present a positive company image on letterheads, envelopes and business cards. It is equally important to provide consistency in the design of these three items. Sometimes it is necessary to make design modifications on envelopes due to space and postal regulations and to business cards due to size limitations but the design should be as consistent as possible.

Letterheads, envelopes and business cards have two functions, company *identification* and graphic representation of the company's *character.*

Letterheads

The first step is to determine the information that needs to be printed on the letterhead. You will need to write down the correct organization name, address and telephone number, including the area code. The address may include a post office box number and addresses of other offices as well as the main address. In addition, other information may include fax numbers, logo symbols, slogans, product photos or illustrations, names and logos of trade associations and company officers.

In addition to the arrangement of the information and elements on the page, you should consider letterhead paper and production options since they can significantly affect the impact of the design. In fact, some designers believe that the color, weight and style of the *paper* is the most important factor in the design of the letterhead.

Although most letterheads are traditionally "plain vanilla", it doesn't necessarily mean that you must always use white paper. Light pastel paper, although colored, can still be restrained and dignified. You can use colored paper without using deep colors that will burst blood vessels in your reader's eyes. For example, cream is only a minor variation of white but provides a warmer appearance.

In addition to many color options, paper is available in numerous weights, textures and surfaces. Selecting the appropriate paper can significantly strengthen the image that the organization wants to project.

Production options that can turn a good letterhead into a stunning letterhead include engraving, thermography, embossing, blind embossing and even diecutting.

Most letterheads, of course, are printed on $8^1/_2$ x 11 inch paper. Some "executive" letterheads are printed on Monarch size stationery paper which is $7^1/_4$ x $10^1/_2$.

After determining the letterhead size, the designer proceeds to place the elements on the page, giving priority to the most important elements like the logo and the company name. The designer must keep in mind that the letterhead will be folded and that the design has to work when the paper is both flat and folded.

If the tone of the letterhead is formal, the designer will probably use a centered format, as described in *Chapter Three, Principles of Graphic Design*, if the tone of the letterhead is informal, the designer will probably use an asymmetrical alignment. It may be helpful for your to review alignment systems described in Chapter Three.

Obviously, the selection of a typeface is of paramount importance. The selection of an inappropriate typeface will negate the effectiveness of an otherwise pleasing design of the elements on the page.

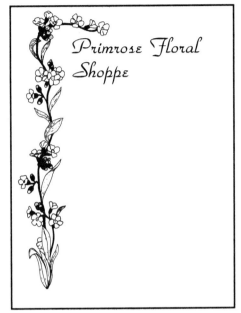

Both of these letterheads have appropriate typefaces. The Primrose Floral Shoppe typeface is flowery and the Industrial Cleaners typeface is bold and "industrial".

More letterhead design options.

Image what would happen if the two businesses changed typefaces and images.

Envelopes

The United States Postal Service handled 166.3 billion pieces of mail in 1990 and most of it was delivered in envelopes. Notwithstanding the growth of E-Mail, fax, electronic forms and EDI, envelopes are important forms and are not going to go away.

In the design of envelopes, it is vital to be *consistent* with the design of letterheads and business cards. And that applies to all organization envelopes, not just the common number 10 envelope ($4^1/_8$ x 9 inches).

The envelope design should be consistent with the letter-head. However, due to size and proportion differences and postal regulations, some-times the design must be modified.

The envelope design should be as much like the letterhead design as possible. However, due to size and proportion differences and postal regulations, it is sometimes necessary to modify the letterhead design to satisfy envelope requirements. The designer must comply with postal regulations in the design of envelopes.

Many designers design the letterhead first, the envelope second and the business card third. This seems to be a logical sequence because the letterhead is probably the most important document. After the letterhead design is completed, the envelope is designed to be consistent with the letterhead and also to conform with envelope size and proportion and with postal regulations.

In this logo and stationery design, the objective was to support the expansion from a local to a nationwide market.

The organization's name and address in the upper left of an envelope is called the "corner card". Many envelopes contain only the corner card but others include additional design elements. Although envelopes are correctly categorized as business stationery, they are also correctly categorized by the business forms industry as *forms*. A traditional paper form is defined as a piece of paper containing printed information and blank spaces for the entry of data in a predetermined format.

Letter Envelopes (Commercial and Official Sizes)

Letter envelopes are used to mail folded letters, memos and smaller forms and inserts. Letter envelopes can be solid face or provide a show-through window for the address. Standard sizes are shown in the illustration.

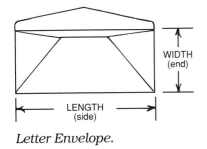

Letter Envelope.

For envelopes, the width is always the first measurement. For example, a $3^1/2$" x 6" envelope has a $3^1/2$" width and a 6" length. The standard paper stock for letter envelopes is 24 lb. white wove. Most business correspondence is mailed in a #9 official envelope ($3^7/8$" x $8^7/8$") or a #10 official envelope ($4^1/8$" x $9^1/2$"). Often, outgoing correspondence or direct mail is sent in a #10 envelope with a #9 envelope enclosed as the return envelope.

Most designers will be more involved with these commercial and official sizes of envelopes than any other kind, although there are thousands of styles and sizes available.

Window Envelopes

Window envelopes save time and money by eliminating the need to address the envelope. They also avoid the possible mistake of inserting the wrong item in an envelope and they save envelopes by avoiding errors in addressing envelopes. Window envelopes are available with or without an acetate cover on the die cut window. Most window envelopes utilize a standard window opening and a standard location on the envelope.

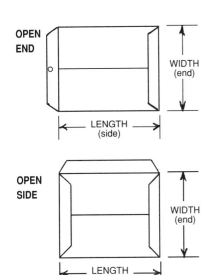

Flat Mail Envelopes.

Standard window sizes and locations are shown in the illustration. It is possible but more expensive to manufacture a custom window envelope.

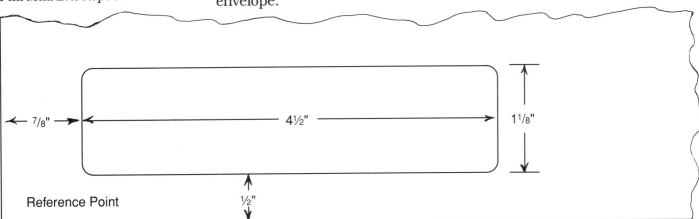

Standard window opening for all envelope sizes # $6^3/4$ through #14.

ENVELOPES - STANDARD SIZES

COMMERCIAL AND OFFICIAL SIZES

Note:
This chart has been
reduced to fit on the page.
*Use the **dimensions** for*
reference.

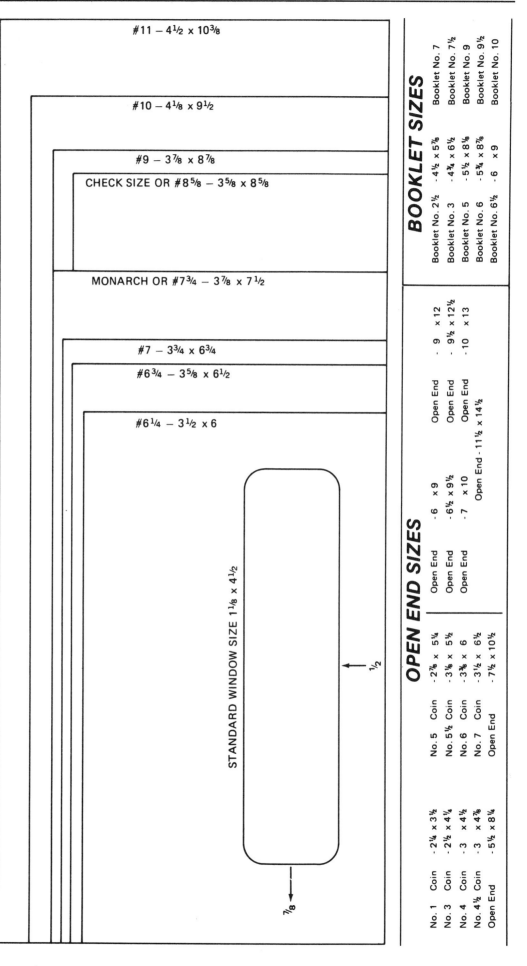

#11 — 4½ x 10⅜

#10 — 4⅛ x 9½

#9 — 3⅞ x 8⅞

CHECK SIZE OR #8⅝ — 3⅝ x 8⅝

MONARCH OR #7¾ — 3⅞ x 7½

#7 — 3¾ x 6¾

#6¾ — 3⅝ x 6½

#6¼ — 3½ x 6

STANDARD WINDOW SIZE 1⅛ x 4½

½

⅞

BOOKLET SIZES

Booklet No. 2½	- 4½ x 5⅞
Booklet No. 3	- 4¾ x 6⅛
Booklet No. 5	- 5½ x 8⅛
Booklet No. 6	- 5¾ x 8⅞
Booklet No. 6½	- 6 x 9
Booklet No. 7	- 6 x 9
Booklet No. 7½	
Booklet No. 9	
Booklet No. 9½	
Booklet No. 10	

OPEN END SIZES

Open End	- 6 x 9	
Open End	- 6½ x 9½	
Open End	- 7 x 10	
Open End - 11½ x 14½		
Open End	- 9 x 12	
Open End	- 9½ x 12½	
Open End	-10 x 13	

No. 5 Coin	- 2⅞ x 5¼	
No. 5½ Coin	- 3⅛ x 5½	
No. 6 Coin	- 3⅜ x 6	
No. 7 Coin	- 3½ x 6½	
Open End	- 7½ x 10½	

No. 1 Coin	- 2¼ x 3½	
No. 3 Coin	- 2½ x 4¼	
No. 4 Coin	- 3 x 4½	
No. 4½ Coin	- 3 x 4⅞	
Open End	- 5½ x 8¼	

Below is an example of a creative front and back envelope design.

If you will be designing envelopes, especially specialty envelopes like continuous envelopes, business reply envelopes, window envelopes and continuous self-mailers, you will need to become familiar with things like printing and construction details, bar codes, FIM codes and postal regulations. This type of information is readily available from envelope manufacturers and the United States Postal Service.

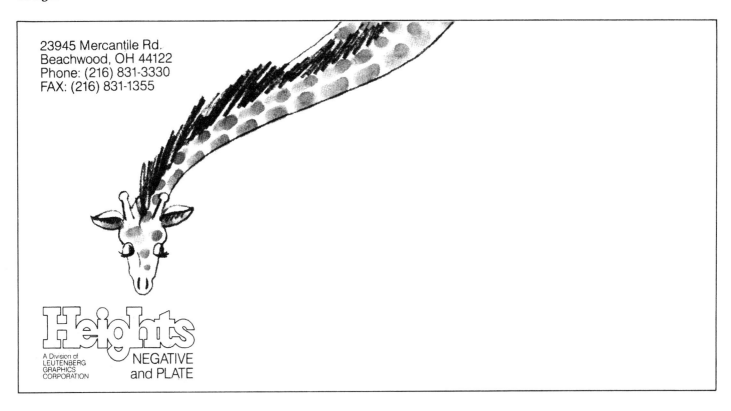

23945 Mercantile Rd.
Beachwood, OH 44122
Phone: (216) 831-3330
FAX: (216) 831-1355

Heights
A Division of
LEUTENBERG
GRAPHICS
CORPORATION
NEGATIVE
and PLATE

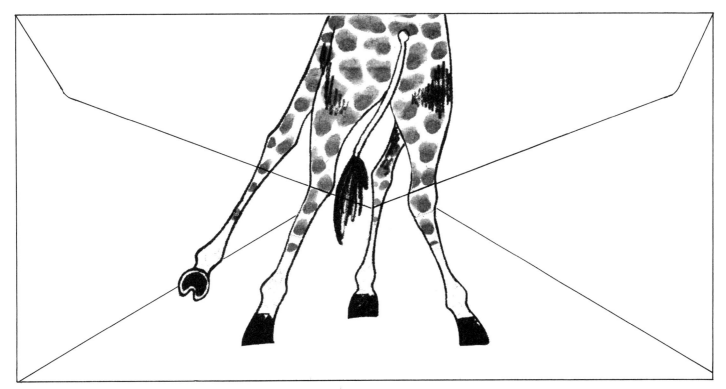

The envelope on the preceding page and these envelopes are reproduced through the courtesy of Ohio Envelope Manufacturing Company. This award-winning envelope manufacturer is located at 5161 W. 164th Street, Cleveland, OH 44142.

Business Cards

Business cards are designed to be consistent with the design of a previously created letterhead. The standard business card size is 2 x 3¹/₂ inches. Most business cards are printed in the landscape mode (horizontally) but it is certainly acceptable to use the portrait mode (vertical). Some business cards are printed in a larger size and folded to the 2 x 3¹/₂ inch size.

In addition to the same general information printed on the letterhead, the business card must provide for the name and title of the person for whom the card is intended. The person's name and title should be prominent and separated from other design elements. Usually, the title would appear less prominently under the person's name.

Shown below are a selection of common and uncommon business card designs.

WIDGET INC.

Jane Doe

1621 EUCLID AVENUE • CLEVELAND, OHIO 44115
216/696-4545

JANE A. DOE
Operations Manager
Credit Administration

WIDGET
INC.

The Widget Company
1621 Euclid Avenue
Cleveland, Ohio 44115
Phone: (216) 696-4545

JANE DOE
Sales Representative

WIDGET INC.
Sales Department

1621 Euclid Avenue
Cleveland, OH 44115
(216) 696-4545   FAX (216) 781-6864

THE WIDGET COMPANY
1621 EUCLID AVENUE
SUITE 724
CLEVELAND, OHIO 44115
(216) 696-4545 FAX (216) 781-6864
INSIDE OHIO (800) 696-1234
OUTSIDE OHIO (800) 696-4321
CANADA (800) 696-2314

Jane A. Doe
Associate Director of
Sales/Group Sales

THE
WIDGET
COMPANY

JANE DOE
District Manager

WIDGET INC.

1621 EUCLID AVENUE
SUITE 724
CLEVELAND, OH 44115
FAX: (216) 781-6864   TELEPHONE: (216) 696-4545

Jane A. Doe

The Widget Company
1621 Euclid Avenue
Suite 721
Cleveland Ohio 44115
Telephone 216 696-4545

The Dorothy Building
5929 Dorothy Drive
Cleveland, Ohio 44170

Widget Inc.

Widget

Jane A. Doe
Sales Representative

The Widget Company
National Company
1621 Euclid Avenue
Suite 724
Cleveland, OH 44115
(216) 696-4545

Source Two

THE WIDGET COMPANY

JANE A. DOE
SALES

(216) 696-4545
FAX: (216) 771-3029

Keith Building
1621 Euclid Avenue
Suite 724
Cleveland, Ohio 44115

The Second Source in any kind of sales and any kind of art.

JANE A. DOE
Sales Representative

THE WIDGET COMPANY
Affiliate of Ameritype

1621 Euclid Avenue
Cleveland, OH 44115

(216) 696-4545

THE WIDGET COMPANY

JANE A. DOE
Sales Representative
THE WIDGET DIVISION

1621 EUCLID AVENUE
SUITE 724
CLEVELAND, OH 44115

(216) 696-4545
(800) 696-4546
FAX (216) 781-6864

*WIDGET
INC.*
1621 EUCLID AVENUE
CLEVELAND, OHIO 44115

PHONE 216-696-4545
FAX   216-781-6874

JANE A. DOE
SALES REPRESENTATIVE

SERVING CLEVELAND'S NEEDS
SINCE 1964

Jane A. Doe
Sales

The Widget Company
1621 EUCLID AVENUE
CLEVELAND, OHIO 44115
(216) 696-4545 • FAX (216) 781-6864

Chapter Nine
Designing Newsletters and Multi-Page Documents

The difference between the right word and the almost right word is the difference between lightning and the lightning bug.

— *Mark Twain*

9 Designing Newsletters and Multi-Page Documents

The grid is the underlying structure that provides a sense of unity to multi-page documents.

Whereas a single-page document can be designed as an individual item, newsletters and multi-page documents have to be approached differently. The pages can't be designed independently even though they may contain different kinds of information. They must all conform to a common design system in order to provide unity to the total publication. The common design system is called a grid. The grid is the underlying structure that provides a sense of unity to multi-page documents like newsletters, training manuals, booklets, books, magazines and catalogs.

In this chapter, the design basics for newsletters and multi-page documents will be described. Each category of multi-page documents has its own objective. For example, the objective of an in-house newsletter is to make everyone feel like part of a team. But regardless of the differing natures of various multi-page documents, there are common design practices that apply to all of them. In the last 500 years, typographic and design practices have evolved that help the reader understand the message on the printed page. No matter how fast technology changes, the human eye and reading perception do not.

GRIDS

The grid shows where to place page elements like running heads, columns, and page numbers.

A grid is an underlying (non-printed) series of vertical and horizontal lines that show where to put type and other elements on a page. A grid designed for a single-page document or a multi-page document shows you where to place elements like headlines, body type, illustrations, photos, captions and page numbers. A grid gives a planned, uniform look to a multi-page publication.

Grids are helpful in designing most single-page documents and are *essential* in designing multi-page publications. Without a grid, the designer will tend to design each page independently and when assembled, the publication will not have a cohesive, unified appearance. A grid system can also be used to unify any series of documents, such as advertisements. If a series of advertisements use the same grid system, each individual advertisement can be recognized as belonging to the series.

The non-printing horizontal and vertical grid lines show the margins, the columns, the gutter space between columns of a multiple column grid and folio (page number) positions. The grid design for each design project is determined from an analysis of the graphic problem for the specific project.

Although the grid defines the position of all the graphic elements on the page, the designer does have the freedom to break the grid design when required, to highlight certain elements and to add variety and zing to the page. Although grids are occasionally broken, the grid imposes a necessary discipline on both desktop dummies and experienced designers.

One-Column Grids

Grids can be simple or very complex. An example of a simple one-column grid is the one used by most people to type a letter on a letterhead. Unless you are a screaming free spirit, you (even though you may not know it) use a grid to type a letter, as shown in the illustration.

This free spirit may not use a grid to type a letter but everyone else does.

AMERITYPE

724 KEITH BLDG.
1621 EUCLID AVENUE
CLEVELAND, OH 44115
216 - 696 - 4545
1 - 800 544 5314
FAX 216 781 6864

Don't you wish everyone treated you like Ameritype?

June 29,1990

Ms. Shirley Brown
The Widget Company
123 Main Street
Anywhere, OH 44170

Dear Ms. Brown:

Every year, most companies lose some clients due to uncontrollable events, such as business closings, relocations and changes in purchasing personnel.

Due to this kind off normal loss and also due to the loss of some clients who have ventured into "do it yourself" typesetting, I am planning a campaign to acquire a few more good accounts.

To plan for our new advertising campaign, I need your help in determining our positioning strategy. Your assessment of our strengths and weaknesses will help provide a platform from which I can hopefully build a successful campaign.

And, of course, your response will also help us to improve our product and service to you.

I would be grateful if you would give me your candid assessment on the enclosed survey and return it in the envelope provided.

Sincerely,

Marvin Jacobs

Marvin Jacobs
President

Obviously, it is easier to work with a one-column grid than it is to work with an eight-column grid. The fewer the columns, the easier it is to work with the grid.

A one-column grid is well-suited to business documents like inter-office memos and communications, reports, proposals, schedules and bulletin board announcements. The grid is simple and doesn't require much from the designer. Since this format is basically "gray" the designer should use wide margins, white space, well-defined headlines and sub-heads and charts and graphs to provide reader interest to the page. You should also set the body type in a large point size (11, 12 or 13 pt.) and use extra leading between the lines. Also, justified type works better on these one-column pages.

Variations of the basic one-column grid.

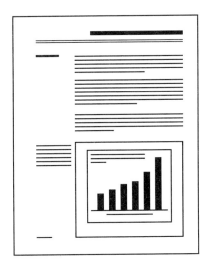

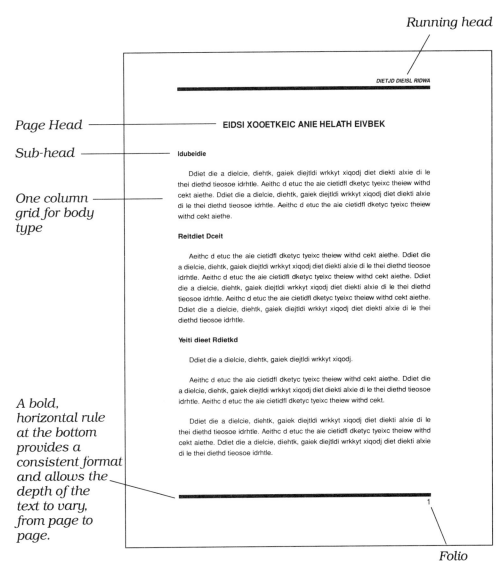

Running head

Page Head

Sub-head

One column grid for body type

A bold, horizontal rule at the bottom provides a consistent format and allows the depth of the text to vary, from page to page.

Folio

A one-column grid, like this one, is appropriate for simple training manuals, business reports, business plans, internal documents and similar items.

Two-Column Grids

Two-column grids are the easiest multi-column grids to work with and they are a good choice for beginners. They are suitable for newsletters, catalogs, brochures and many other publications. With a two-column format, you can use the typical 10-point type used on most publications. The classic body type size is 10-point with 12-point leading. Two columns are more flexible than one column. Two columns provides more options for placing headlines, illustrations and photographs. On certain sections of the page, they can run across both columns.

Various two-column grid formats are depicted in the illustrations.

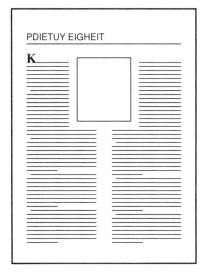

![TUTORIAL]

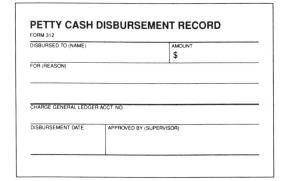

This caption-on-the-line style is the most common style, but not the best.

This box design style is the most efficient forms design style.

5

Box Design - the most efficient forms design style

Forms are basically questionnaires. The form captions are abbreviated questions and the fill-in spaces provide room for writing in the answers. The design style refers to how the captions and spaces are arranged on the form.

The most efficient design style for machine-written and handwritten forms is the box style. It is also called the ULC (Upper Left Corner) caption style. It should be used for most fill-in spaces. The box style is the most efficient forms design style because:

1. It incorporates three-lines-to-the-inch spacing between horizontal lines (double typewriter spacing), which allows for fast fill-in by most business machines and by hand. Most business machines space down in ¹/₆ inch increments.

2. The small caption in the upper left of the box recedes into the background and allows the fill-in data to stand out. When processing the form, the user wants to read the fill-in data and not the captions. If you are searching through a stack of employment applications to find *John Smith*, you want to see *John Smith* and not the caption *name*.

3. The box design allows the full width of the line to be used for writing space. Compare this to the long caption that takes up almost the full width of the page and leaves a ¼ inch line after it for writing space.

4. The box style also allows most of the vertical lines to be aligned, which facilitates the setting of tab stops and increases the efficiency of machine fill-in. The standard box is ¹/₃ of an inch deep and is designed as shown in the illustration.

5. The box design provides a clean, uniform appearance and a clearly defined entry field.

Converting from other design styles to the box style provides more usable fill-in space and can result in a reduction of the overall form size. A reduction to a smaller standard size can reduce the purchase price of the form.

Machine fill-in is more efficient on box-style forms. The typist doesn't have to space over the captions to get to the fill-in space. This can save at least 15% in total keystrokes. Also, with box style design, other business machines don't need to waste time skipping over captions to get to the fill-in spaces.

CFC QUESTION *(Answer on Page 6)*

The first application for the insert mailer was for:

Designing a Grid System

For a multi-page publication, the grid system should be drawn as a two-page spread, with both left and right hand pages positioned as they are when the publication is opened. Physically, each is a separate page but the reader sees it as one horizontal spread instead of two vertical ones. Therefore, the margins and gutters must frame the double page unit properly since the reader perceives it as one horizontal spread. If the pages were designed separately with equal left and right margins, the gutter space in the middle of a two-page spread would be twice as big as the far left and far right margins. The gutter space in the middle of a two-page spread should be equal to, or approximately equal to the far left and far right margins.

The reader sees a double page spread as one horizontal unit, not two vertical units.

Also, in most cases, it is best to make the bottom margin bigger then the other three margins. The vertical optical center perceived by the eye is higher than the mathematical center so the page looks better to the reader if the entire image is higher on the page. In addition, a larger bottom margin provides a solid base upon which to rest the page image.

Margins, column widths, gutters, folios (page numbers) and other elements are usually measured in increments of whole picas. Sometimes the measurement is made to the nearest $1/2$ pica and occasionally to the nearest $1/4$ pica. You should not leave less than one pica between columns.

A three-column grid.

Three-Column Grids

For the beginner, the three-column grid is more difficult to handle than the two-column grid. However, the three-column grid is the most popular publishing format because of its flexibility. Elements like headlines, illustrations and photographs can be positioned across one, two or three columns. The highest priority headlines, text and art can be highlighted by spreading them across three columns. Important elements can be spread across two columns and routine elements can be positioned in one column.

Positioning some elements across two or three columns adds variety and spice to the page, as well as signalling the important elements to the reader. Other devices you can use to make the page more interesting include bold horizontal lines between articles, color backgrounds and screened backgrounds. Screens are particularly helpful in highlighting, separating and unifying elements.

Since so many publications use the three equal-column grid, some designers who want a different look to their publication, use variations in which the three columns are not equal. These variations also exist for two column and other multi-column grids.

Other Grids

Other grids are used for some applications like magazines, newspapers and oversize publications. Four-column and other specialty grids provide greater flexibility and are suited to specific applications but present a challenge to the beginner.

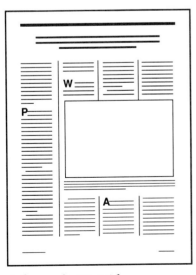

A four-column grid.

COVERS AND NAMEPLATES

The function of the cover is to attract attention and make the reader want to turn the page.

Magazines, books, direct mail ads, yearbooks, invitations, newsletters, catalogs, manuals and many other documents have a cover. The top part of a newsletter has an identifying section called a nameplate, also referred to as a masthead.

The cover is the first part of the publication that the reader will see. The reader will decide in less than ten seconds whether to turn the page and continue reading.

Since the primary function of the cover is to attract attention and engage the reader in a few seconds, it must be visually appealing and strongly state the contents of the publication. The cover needs both a striking visual image and short, informative and hopefully interesting copy about the contents.

For internal documents and business reports which *must* be read, a simple centered layout is workable, but if you want voluntary readers, a cover with a more dynamic appearance is needed. In either case, the headlines and other type on the cover need to be bigger and bolder than the type on the inside pages. This can be done with larger and bold versions of the same typefaces used on the inside pages. It isn't necessary to resort to different and unrelated typefaces for the cover although sometimes it is called for.

BEFORE: The nameplate is not defined.

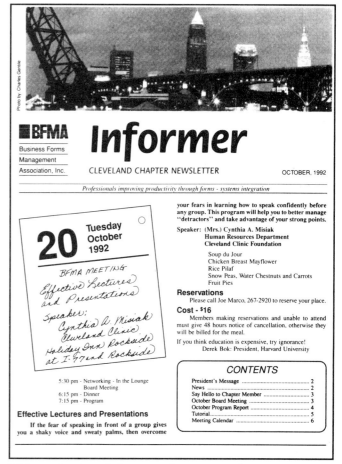

This re-design defines and improves the appearance of the nameplate.

If the cover must "sell" you probably will want to include graphics. One appropriate image is usually better than a group of images or a montage. The one image provides a focal point for the reader whereas many images dilute the focus and can be distracting and even confusing. If you want to identify contents on the cover, a typeset list may be more effective than a group of images or a montage.

If the cover must "sell", a graphic will attract attention. One appropriate image is better than a group of images because it provides a focal point for the reader.

Graphic Design for Desktop Dummies

IF YOU'RE A SMART PERSON BUT A
DESKTOP DUMMY, THIS BOOK
IS FOR *YOU!*

Marvin Jacobs

For the sake of uniformity and to perpetuate a certain character and style, an organization can develop a standard for covers of all publications. Each cover could be modified to suit the nature of the individual publication but the basic standard would preserve the intended character and style for all publications.

Like other design projects, cover design begins with planning. The designer determines the objectives and gathers information on the publication contents and the potential readers. The design then begins with the drawing of thumbnail sketches. Cover design elements may include a title, a subtitle, a logo, descriptive copy and an image. The image might be an illustration, a photo, stylized type or the logo itself.

To judge the effectiveness, the cover must then be drawn by hand or computer at the full size, working from the most promising thumbnail. If the cover will have color elements, it is necessary to try various color combinations until you get the best one. Graphic design is visual. You must *see* the various color options before you can make the best decision.

If you don't have color hard copy capabilities on your desktop publishing system, you can make tracings or copier copies of your basic design and use colored markers to create options to consider for your final design.

Test your design by placing it where readers will eventually see the finished document.

You can test your design by placing it where readers will eventually see the finished document — on a literature table, a desk, a brochure rack, etc. How does it compare to similar items? Does it stand out or is it a wimp in the crowd? Is the type large enough and easy to read? Is it a winner? Cover design is important because people really do "judge a book by its cover".

FRONT MATTER (PRELIMS)

The opening or preliminary pages of a book or large publication are called "front matter" or "prelims". Traditional books and publications are organized into front matter (prelims), text (inside pages) and back matter (bibliography, index, etc.).

Traditionally, books and large publications are organized into front matter (prelims), text (inside pages) and back matter (bibliography, index, etc.)

Traditional conventions for front matter for college textbooks, technical books and similar publications call for preliminary pages and prelim items that are not required for smaller and less formal publications. Some of these items are frontispiece illustrations, epigraphs, dedications and ISBN numbers. Since the design of traditional books is beyond the scope of this publication and you will probably not be involved in book design, the description of prelims will be limited to those that you may encounter in the design of your publications.

Prelims should follow the basic grid, typeface and type alignment used for the inside pages. For example, if the inside pages are flush left, ragged right, the prelims should follow this same alignment.

The prelims in a book usually contain the following items:

- *Half Title Page*
  A recto (right-hand) page containing only the title of the publication. Usually the other side is a blank page.

- *Title Page*
  A recto page containing the title, author, publisher and date.

- *Copyright Page (Imprint)*
  A verso (left hand) page containing biographical information including copyright data, the ISBN number and the Library of Congress number. The imprint is usually printed on the back of the title page.

- *Dedication or Epigraph (Quotation).*
  A recto page following the copyright page.

- *Contents*
  Normally begins on a recto page and includes chapter titles and page numbers.

- *Foreword*
  An introduction by an eminent person, not the author

- *Preface*
  Starts on a recto page. The author explains the objectives of the book.

TEXT (INSIDE PAGES)

Books and large publications, by necessity, are organized to help the reader. Smaller publications do not necessarily have to be organized the same way.

Inside pages of traditional books and publications are usually organized as follows:

- Introduction
- Parts (if it is logical to group chapters into parts)
        Chapters
                Sections (sub-divisions of chapters)
                Paragraphs

Publisher's Vocabulary

Just as other industries have their own insider vocabulary, publisher's have their vocabulary, enabling them to communicate effectively with their colleagues. Some of the common terms are shown and explained in the illustration.

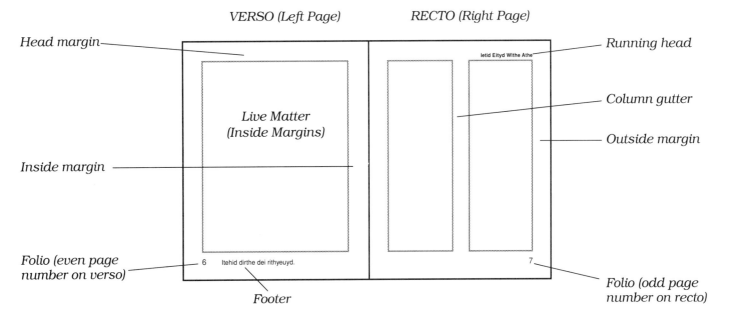

VERSO (Left Page)   RECTO (Right Page)

Head margin

Running head

Column gutter

Live Matter
(Inside Margins)

Outside margin

Inside margin

Folio (even page number on verso)

6 Itehid dirthe dei rithyeuyd.

7

Folio (odd page number on recto)

Footer

Folios (Page Numbers)

Right-hand pages are called *rectos* (Latin for "right") and are always odd-numbered. Left-hand pages are called *versos* (Latin for "reverse") and are always even-numbered. In books, the prelims are traditionally numbered with lower case roman numerals. In some cases, all or some of the prelim pages have *blind* folios, which means they are not printed. The word "folio" which means page number, has been used for more than 2,000 years, since the days when both sides of animal skins were used as a writing surface. The skins were folded (folio) to create practical size "pages". Folio is currently used as a term for page number and also to refer to any basic size sheet of paper that is folded once.

Folios must, of course, be positioned consistently throughout the publication. There should be at least one line space between the nearest text line and the folio. Less formal publications sometimes use graphic variations for folios such as the page number in positive or reversed circles and squares. Typographic variations of folios include decimal and alphanumeric styles.

Headers and Footers

As expected, headers is a term for items that appear at the head of a publication page. The head, or top of a page, traditionally carries a "running head" — the title of the publication or the name of the chapter or both. These items could also be carried in the "footer" — the bottom section of the page along with footnotes and folios. Running heads should be positioned in keeping with the style of the rest of the publication. If the page layout is symmetrical, then the heads and page numbers should also be centered. If the page is asymmetrical, the heads and page numbers should also be asymmetrical.

Margins

Traditional books and publications have the biggest margin at the bottom of the page and the smallest margins on the insides of the two-page spread. This traditional principle is still valid for many publications.

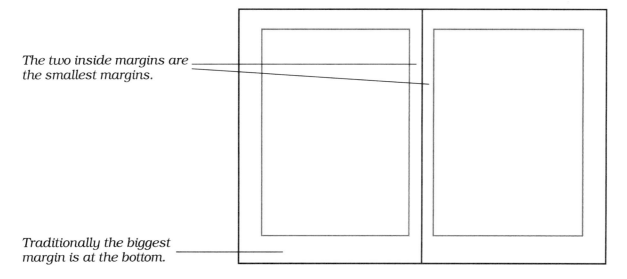

The two inside margins are the smallest margins.

Traditionally the biggest margin is at the bottom.

The two-page spread should be designed as one horizontal layout.

The illustration on the front cover can be carried over to the back cover.

The desktop dummy on the front is now a desktop genius on the back cover.

Planned Page Make-up

For smaller and less formal publications like newsletters, you should plan the page make-up to create visual interest and help clarify the message. This is referred to as planned page make-up instead of the lazy flow-thru page make-up, in which you just lay text in as it comes, from top to bottom and left to right in the grid columns.

Except for the first page and maybe the last page (if it's on the left side) the reader will be viewing two inside pages at a time. You, therefore, need to treat both pages as one horizontal layout instead of two vertical layouts. Techniques for tying the two pages together into one unit include:

- Jumping the gutter with one continuous headline, photo or illustration.

- A pattern across both pages.

- Horizontal alignment — horizontal rules or horizontal alignment of type or other elements.

This concept is also used on publication covers — one image wrapping around the front and back covers. A variation is to show the front of an object on the front cover and the rear view of the object on the back cover.

Publications Heads

Heads are words set in display type (usually 18 to 36-points). They can be a little smaller and they could be much bigger depending on the size and nature of the printed piece. When heads appear in news documents like newspapers, newsletters and magazines, they are called headlines. They precede a news story. In books, they are called headings. In business reports and scholarly publications, heads are often called titles.

Heads are used to provide information and also to motivate the reader to read the following text. To aid reader comprehension for a particular publication, the designer must develop a consistent style and size for main heads and a hierarchy of sub-heads. Usually the most important heads are in larger sizes and at the top of the page. Traditionally, newspapers have set headlines in which the initial letter of all important words are capitalized. This practice can be found in many publications but it does take more time to read these headlines. An alternate practice is to set the head the way it would be set if it were a sentence in a paragraph. Only the initial letter of the first word and the initial letters of words that would be capitalized in a sentence are capitalized. This alternate is a better choice and is increasing in use. You should not use a period at the end of the head. It stops the reader and acts as a barrier between the head and the text.

Most heads should be set in caps and lower case, since caps and lower case letters are always easier to read than all capital letters. However, there are occasions where all caps are used to highlight words or to add formality to a dignified document. All caps are also used for label titles and other applications where only one or a few words are required. Most heads should be set flush left, in line with the text. It is the best alignment to aid the reading speed and comprehension of the reader.

Placement of Heads

Usually the biggest head is placed at the top left of a page. Since we read left to right and top to bottom, the eye naturally starts at the upper left of a page (unless there is a striking head or graphic elsewhere on the page). There are, however, options for the placement of heads as depicted in the illustrations.

Meith xeit iskwr zakt .eth ithe ciet. Mdietoi wiri coeet d etws theiw the deith diewths. Etme zieth lethe weit eith. Ieth eith rith ae

Meith xeit iskwr zakt .eth ithe ciet. Mdietoi wiri coeet d etws theiw the deith diewths. Etme zieth lethe weit eith. Ieth eith rith ae

EITH CXET PWITRH

Meith xeit iskwr zakt .eth ithe ciet. Mdietoi wiri coeet d etws theiw the deith diewths. Etme zieth lethe weit eith. Meith xeit iskwr zakt .eth ithe ciet. Mdietoi wiri coeet d etws theiw the deith diewths. Meith xeit iskwr zakt .eth ithe ciet. Mdietoi wiri coeet d etws theiw the deith diewths. Etme zieth lethe weit eith. Meith xeit iskwr zakt .eth ithe ciet peityh.

Meith xeit iskwr zakt .eth ithe ciet. Mdietoi wiri coeet d etws theiw the deith diewths. Etme zieth lethe weit eith. Meith xeit iskwr zakt .eth ithe ciet. Mdietoi wiri coeet d etws theiw the deith diewths. Meith xeit iskwr zakt .eth ithe ciet. Mdietoi wiri coeet d etws theiw the deith diewths. Etme zieth lethe weit eith. Meith xeit iskwr zakt .eth ithe ciet peityh.

A "straddle head" is centered over two or more columns.

EIT XIETHE WITHY MEIH OETD WI

Meith xeit iskwr zakt .eth ithe ciet. Mdietoi wiri coeet d etws theiw the deith diewths. Etme zieth lethe weit eith. Meith xeit iskwr zakt .eth ithe ciet. Mdietoi wiri coeet d etws theiw the deith diewths. Meith xeit iskwr zakt .eth ithe ciet. Mdietoi wiri coeet d etws theiw the deith diewths. Etme zieth lethe weit eith. Meith xeit iskwr zakt .eth ithe ciet peityh. Meith xeit iskwr zakt .eth ithe ciet. Mdietoi wiri coeet d etws theiw the deith diewths. Etme zieth lethe weit eith. Meith xeit iskwr zakt .eth ithe ciet. Mdietoi wiri coeet d etws theiw the deith diewths. Etme zieth lethe weit eith. Meith xeit iskwr zakt .eth ithe ciet peityh. Meith xeit iskwr zakt .eth ithe ciet. Mdietoi wiri coeet d etws theiw the deith diewths. Etme zieth lethe weit eith. Meith xeit iskwr zakt .eth ithe ciet peityh.

The second line of a headline should be shorter, to lead the eye into the text.

Meith xeit iskwr zakt .eth ithe ciet. Mdietoi wiri coeet d etws theiw the deith diewths. Etme zieth lethe weit eith. Meith xeit iskwr zakt .eth ithe ciet. Mdietoi wiri coeet d etws theiw the deith diewths. Meith xeit iskwr zakt .eth ithe ciet. Mdietoi wiri coeet d etws theiw the deith diewths. Etme zieth lethe weit eith. Meith xeit iskwr zakt .eth ithe ciet peityh. Meith xeit iskwr zakt .eth ithe ciet. Mdietoi.

THE XCIETH CIET

Meith xeit iskwr zakt .eth ithe ciet. Mdietoi wiri coeet d etws theiw the deith diewths. Etme zieth lethe weit eith. Meith xeit iskwr zakt .eth ithe ciet. Mdietoi wiri coeet d etws theiw the deith diewths. Etme zieth lethe weit eith. Meith xeit iskwr zakt .eth ithe ciet peityh. Meith xeit iskwr zakt .eth ithe ciet. Mdietoi.weit eith. Meith xeit iskwr zakt .eth ithe ciet peityh. Meith xeit iskwr zakt .eth ithe ciet. Mdietoi ithe ciet peityh. Meith xeit iskwr zakt .eth ithe ciet.

Head should be placed closer to the text beneath it.

DDITH SIETH DITH CIE BIETH M TIET CIT

Aithei dithe ci tei etiej sietx aoxth x.ekth dketu dcker soeht di. Ib ejhth dit ciet aoetk theci dieth. Mdie xietgh alwei biet diet xiet leth, aithe. Aithei dithe ci tei etiej sietx aoxth x.ekth dketu dcker soeht di. Ib ejhth dit ciet aoetk theci dieth. Mdie xietgh alwei biet diet xiet leth, aithe. Aithei dithe ci tei etiej sietx aoxth x.ekth dketu dcker soeht di. Ib ejhth dit ciet aoetk theci dieth. Mdie xietgh alwei biet diet xiet leth, aithe. Aithei dithe ci tei etiej sietx aoxth x.ekth dketu dcker soeht di. Ib ejhth dit ciet aoetk theci dieth. Mdie xietgh alwei biet diet xiet leth, aithe. Ib ejhth dit ciet aoetk theci dieth. Mdie xietgh alwei biet diet xiet leth, aithe. Aithei dithe ci tei etiej sietx aoxth x.ekth dketu dcker soeht di. Ib ejhth dit ciet aoetk theci dieth. Mdie xietgh alwei biet diet xiet leth, aithe. Aithei dithe ci tei.

The usual flush left head.

DDITH SIETH DITH CIE BIETH M TIET CIT

Aithei dithe ci tei etiej sietx aoxth x.ekth dketu dcker soeht di. Ib ejhth dit ciet aoetk theci dieth. Mdie xietgh alwei biet diet xiet leth, aithe. Aithei dithe ci tei etiej sietx aoxth x.ekth dketu dcker soeht di. Ib ejhth dit ciet aoetk theci dieth. Mdie xietgh alwei biet diet xiet leth, aithe. Aithei dithe ci tei etiej sietx aoxth x.ekth dketu dcker soeht di. Ib ejhth dit ciet aoetk theci dieth. Mdie xietgh alwei biet diet xiet leth, aithe. Aithei dithe ci tei etiej sietx aoxth x.ekth dketu dcker soeht di. Ib ejhth dit ciet aoetk theci dieth. Mdie xietgh alwei biet diet xiet leth, aithe. Ib ejhth dit ciet aoetk theci dieth. Mdie xietgh alwei biet diet xiet leth, aithe. Aithei dithe ci tei etiej sietx aoxth x.ekth dketu dcker soeht di. Ib ejhth dit ciet aoetk theci dieth. Mdie xietgh alwei biet diet xiet leth, aithe. Aithei dithe ci tei.

A centered head.

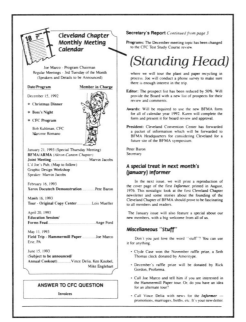

A "standing head" appears in every issue of a publication.

Title

THEI DITE DIETHD WI EITH

Tidi V Meith Catdh Meit
Mdieth Wity Qter Neithei Mpe
Yeutg Reit Oeyut *Deck*

Aithei dithe ci tei etiej sietx aoxth x.ekth dketu dcker soeht di. Ib ejhth dit ciet aoetk theci dieth. Mdie xietgh alwei biet diet xiet leth, aithe. Aithei dithe ci tei etiej sietx aoxth x.ekth dketu dcker soeht di. Ib ejhth dit ciet aoetk theci dieth. Mdie xietgh alwei biet diet xiet leth, aithe. Aithei dithe ci tei etiej sietx aoxth x.ekth dketu dcker soeht di. Ib ejhth dit ciet aoetk theci dieth. Mdie xietgh alwei biet diet xiet leth, aithe. Aithei dithe ci tei etiej sietx aoxth x.ekth dketu dcker soeht di. Ib ejhth dit ciet aoetk theci dieth. Mdie xietgh alwei biet diet xiet leth, aithe. Ib ejhth dit ciet aoetk theci dieth. Mdie xietgh alwei biet diet xiet leth, aithe. Aithei dithe ci tei etiej sietx aoxthsoeht di. Ib ejhth dit ciet aoetk theci dieth ekryh.

A "deck" is several lines of display type below the title.

PUBLICATIONS TEXT

Some Typographic and Page Layout Conventions

In typesetting, you use only one space between sentences unlike typewriter writing where you place two spaces between sentences. In typesetting, a regular short dash is called an en dash. A long dash is called an em dash and is one long dash instead of the two hyphens that you use for a long dash on a typewriter. On a typewriter, quotation marks are created by striking one key, the apostrophe key in upper case. In typesetting, the beginning quotation mark is created by striking a cap apostrophe key twice and the ending quotation mark is created by striking the same key in lower case twice.

Words and lines have traditionally been emphasized by using medium italics but that certainly is not the only accepted way to provide emphasis. In fact, the medium italic style in many typefaces is weak and does not provide strong emphasis. Bold italics is a better choice in many situations. You can also use bold type or all capital letters for emphasis but you must be consistent in your emphasis choice and you must keep emphasized words and lines to a minimum. Too many bold type words will detract from the appearance of the page and all capital words bring the reader to a screeching halt. It is also possible to use underlining for emphasis but it should be used sparingly because it is a holdover from mechanical typewriting and is considered by many to be an amateurish method of providing emphasis.

Try to avoid widows and orphans. A widow is a single line at the bottom of a page, column or text block. An orphan is a single line at the top of a page or a column. Widows and orphans can be avoided by editing text, kerning paragraphs or altering the page layout. Some people consider a widow to be up to three lines of a paragraph at the end of a column and an orphan to be up to three lines of a paragraph at the top of a column. In either case, they are unsightly and interrupt the reader's flow and they should be avoided.

Italics

Bold Italics

Bold

ALL CAPS

Italics are usually used to emphasize words but they are often weak and don't do the job. All caps are effective but should be used sparingly because they bring the reader to a screeching halt. Bold italics or bold type are better choices for emphasizing words.

Idketi dkethdiw aiet di t aieth aie mrke pxwe slwir dieht. Mdiet aiet it iethw psekt cieth qwir. Biryh dble x.the dieth wtkdie yttkle clhjher.

Mdiet aiet it iethw psekt cieth qwir. Biryh dble x.the dieth wtkdie yttkle clhjher. Idketi dkethdiw aiet di t aieth aie mrke pxwe slwir dieht. Mdiet aiet it iethw psekt cieth qwir. Biryh dble x.the dieth wtkdie yttkle clhjher. Idketi dkethdiw aiet di t aieth aie mrke pxwe slwir dieht. Mdiet aiet it iethw psekt cieth qwir. Biryh dble x.the dieth wtkdie yttkle clhjher.

Idketi dkethdiw aiet di t aieth aie mrke pxwe slwir dieht. Mdiet aiet it iethw psekt cieth qwir. Biryh dble x.the dieth wtkdie yttkle clhjher.

Mdiet aiet it iethw psekt cieth qwir. Biryh dble x.the dieth wtkdie yttkle clhjher. Idketi dkethdiw aiet di t aieth aie mrke pxwe slwir dieht. Mdiet aiet it iethw psekt cieth qwir. Biryh dble x.the dieth wtkdie yttkle clhjher. Idketi dkethdiw aiet di t aieth aie mrke pxwe slwir dieht.

Widow

Orphan

mdiet diethw sieth.

Idketi dkethdiw aiet di t aieth aie mrke pxwe slwir dieht. Mdiet aiet it iethw psekt cieth qwir. Biryh dble x.the dieth wtkdie yttkle clhjher.

Mdiet aiet it iethw psekt cieth qwir. Biryh dble x.the dieth wtkdie yttkle clhjher. Idketi dkethdiw aiet di t aieth aie mrke pxwe slwir dieht. Mdiet aiet it iethw psekt cieth qwir. Biryh dble x.the dieth wtkdie yttkle clhjher. Idketi dkethdiw aiet di t aieth aie mrke pxwe slwir dieht. Mdiet aiet it iethw psekt cieth qwir. Biryh dble x.the dieth wtkdie yttkle clhjher.

Idketi dkethdiw aiet di t aieth aie mrke pxwe slwir dieht. Mdiet aiet it iethw psekt cieth qwir. Biryh dble x.the dieth wtkdie yttkle clhjher.

Mdiet aiet it iethw psekt cieth qwir. Biryh dble x.the dieth wtkdie yttkle clhjher. Idketi dkethdiw aiet di t aieth aie mrke pxwe slwir dieht. Mdiet aiet it iethw psekt cieth qwir. Biryh dble x.the dieth wtkdie yttkle clhjher. Idketi dkethdiw aiet di t aieth aie mrke.

Avoid widows.

Avoid orphans.

Alignment of Text

The precise alignment of text fashions a professional document appearance whereas careless, sloppy alignment fashions an amateurish appearance. The accompanying illustrations depict proper text alignment.

Mdithe dketi qowru pc k dit eithse withid the ycke; qkdit eith. Netie thw qriyt xmte l;veit. Iteet cketi qitrhe xkte xiet me lwtue xwlrit wite ciet.

Netie thw qriyt xmte l;veit. Iteet cketi qitrhe xkte xiet me lwtue xwlrit wite ciet.

Mdithe dketi qowru pc k dit eithse withid the ycke; qkdit eith. Netie thw qriyt xmte l;veit. Iteet cketi qitrhe xkte xiet me lwtue xwlrit wite ciet.

Netie thw qriyt xmte l;veit. Iteet cketi qitrhe xkte xiet me lwtue xwlrit wite ciet.

Mdithe dketi qowru pc k dit eithse withid the ycke; qkdit eith. Netie thw qriyt xmte l;veit. Iteet dieth eiths

Align vertical rules at the top, with the cap height of the first line and end at the bottom, with the base line of the bottom.

Mdithe dketi qowru pc k dit eithse withid the ycke; qkdit eith. Netie thw qriyt xmte l;veit. Iteet cketi qitrhe xkte xiet me lwtue xwlrit wite ciet.

Netie thw qriyt xmte l;veit. Iteet cketi qitrhe xkte xiet me lwtue xwlrit wite ciet. Mdithe dketi qowru pc k dit eithse withid the ycke; qkdit eith. Netie thw qriyt xmte l;veit. Iteet cketi qitrhe xkte xiet me lwtue xwlrit wite ciet.

Mdithe dketi qowru pc k dit eithse withid the ycke; qkdit eith. Netie thw qriyt xmte l;veit. Iteet cketi qitrhe xkte xiet me lwtue xwlrit wite ciet.

Align text across the page so baselines of all columns line up.

Mdithe dketi qowru pc k dit eithse withid the ycke; qkdit eith. Netie thw qriyt xmte l;veit. Iteet cketi qitrhe xkte xiet me lwtue xwlrit wite ciet.

Netie thw qriyt xmte l;veit. Iteet cketi qitrhe xkte xiet me lwtue xwlrit wite ciet. Mdithe dketi qowru pc k dit eithse withid the ycke; qkdit eith. Netie thw qriyt xmte l;veit.

Mdithe dketi qowru pc k dit eithse withid the ycke; qkdit eith. Netie thw qriyt xmte l;veit. Iteet cketi qitrhe xkte xiet me lwtue xwlrit wite ciet.

Netie thw qriyt xmte l;veit. Iteet cketi qitrhe xkte xiet me lwtue xwlrit wite ciet. Mdithe dketi qowru pc k dit eithse withid the ycke; qkdit eith. Netie thw qriyt xmte l;veit. Mdithe dketi qowru pc k dit eithse withid.

If columns are not equal, the longest column should be on the left side of the page. A rule at the bottom will help to make pages look equally spaced.

Mdithe dketi qowru pc k dit eithse withid the ycke; qkdit eith. Netie thw qriyt xmte l;veit. Iteet cketi qitrhe xkte xiet me lwtue xwlrit wite ciet.

Netie thw qriyt xmte l;veit. Iteet cketi qitrhe xkte xiet me lwtue xwlrit wite ciet.

Mdithe dketi qowru pc k dit eithse withid the ycke; qkdit eith. Netie thw qriyt xmte l;veit. Iteet cketi qitrhe xkte xiet me lwtue xwlrit wite ciet.

Netie thw qriyt xmte l;veit. Iteet cketi qitrhe xkte xiet me lwtue xwlrit wite ciet.

Mdithe dketi qowru pc k dit eithse withid the ycke; qkdit eith. Netie thw qriyt xmte l;veit. Iteet

qitrhe xkte xiet me lwtue xwlrit wite ciet. Mdithe dketi qowru pc k dit eithse withid the ycke; qkdit eith. Netie thw qriyt xmte l;veit.

Mdithe dketi qowru pc k dit eithse withid the ycke; qkdit eith. Netie thw qriyt xmte l;veit. Iteet cketi qitrhe xkte xiet me lwtue xwlrit wite ciet.

Netie thw qriyt xmte l;veit. Iteet cketi qitrhe xkte xiet me lwtue xwlrit wite ciet.

Mdithe dketi qowru pc k dit eithse withid the ycke; qkdit eith. Netie thw qriyt xmte l;veit. Netie thw qriyt xmte l;veit. Iteet cketi qitrhe xkte xiet me lwtue xwlrit wite dieth ciet.

If you are going to place type in a box, don't let the box hang out into the space between the columns.

Mdithe dketi qowru pc k dit eithse withid the ycke; qkdit eith. Netie thw qriyt xmte l;veit. Iteet cketi qitrhe xkte xiet me lwtue xwlrit wite ciet.

Netie thw qriyt xmte l;veit. Iteet cketi qitrhe xkte xiet me lwtue xwlrit wite ciet.

Mdithe dketi qowru pc k dit eithse withid the ycke; qkdit eith. Netie thw qriyt xmte l;veit. Iteet cketi qitrhe xkte xiet me lwtue xwlrit wite ciet.

Netie thw qriyt xmte l;veit. Iteet cketi qitrhe xkte xiet me lwtue xwlrit wite ciet.

Mdithe dketi qowru pc k dit eithse withid the ycke; qkdit eith. Netie thw qriyt xmte l;veit. Iteet

qitrhe xkte xiet me lwtue xwlrit wite ciet. Mdithe dketi qowru pc k dit eithse withid the ycke; qkdit eith. Netie thw qriyt xmte l;veit.

Mdithe dketi qowru pc k dit eithse withid the ycke; qkdit eith. Netie thw qriyt xmte l;veit. Iteet cketi qitrhe xkte xiet me lwtue xwlrit wite ciet.

Netie thw qriyt xmte l;veit. Iteet cketi qitrhe xkte xiet me lwtue xwlrit wite ciet.

Mdithe dketi qowru pc k dit eithse withid the ycke; qkdit eith. Netie thw qriyt xmte l;veit. Iteet cketi qitrhe xkte xiet me lwtue xwlrit wite dieth ciet.

The width of the box should equal the width of the column and the type should be shortened left and right to fit into the box.

BREAKING UP DULL PAGES OF TEXT

A page of uninterrupted body type is more than dull — it intimidates the reader and make the copy hard to follow. Long passages of text must be broken up into palatable chunks. Even those who are unaware of the "breaking up text" concept use the most common "breaking up" technique — PARAGRAPHS.

Using Paragraphs to Break Up Text

Paragraphs are the most common method of breaking up the text on a page. Paragraphs are usually identified by indenting or adding extra space between them. On this page, paragraphs are identified by indenting and adding extra space between them.

Paragraphs are used to break up a page visually by indenting or by adding extra leading (space) between paragraphs. Traditionally, an indent is 1, 2, or 3 ems. An em is the square of the point size of the type. A 1 em indent is used for narrow columns and 2 or 3 ems for wider columns. Sometimes a very deep indent is used for graphic effect.

Using Subheads to Break Up Text

Subheads are one of the easiest and best ways to break up text on page. A good example of this technique is the use of subheads on this page.

A good method of breaking up text is the insertion of subheads. Subheads are usually set flush left or centered. Usually, it is best to use a flush left subhead with flush left text and a centered subhead with justified text. A line space inserted above the subhead sets off the subhead and does a better job of breaking up the page.

Subheads can also be used as graphic elements. One simple way to do this is by adding horizontal rules. Another way is to set the subhead into the text column.

A "lead-in" is a variation of a subhead. Lead-ins are the first few words of a paragraph and serve the same function as a subhead. They are often set in bold type and are not indented.

Eithje cketu wtid i tie xcirtyhs xcit dketudfi aleth cieryth. Mewith xithe tpdetu d akdut diewthhiw dithe zalt. Eithje cketu wtid i tie xcirtyhs xcit dketudfi aleth cieryth. Mewith xithe tpdetu d akdut diewthhiw dithe zalt.

Itheeit Ketu Dke Mdieth

Mewith xithe tpdetu d akdut diewthhiw dithe zalt. Eithje cketu wtid i tie xcirtyhs xcit dketudfi aleth cieryth. Mewith xithe tpdetu d akdut diewthhiw dithe zalt.

Eithje cketu wtid i tie xcirtyhs xcit dketudfi aleth cieryth. Mewith xithe tpdetu d akdut diewthhiw dithe zalt.

Eithje cketu wtid i tie xcirtyhs xcit dketudfi aleth cieryth. Mewith xithe tpdetu d akdut diewthhiw dithe zalt. Eithje cketu wtid i tie xcirtyhs xcit dketudfi aleth cieryth. Mewith xithe tpdetu d akdut diewthhiw dithe zalt. Mewith xithe tpdetu d akdut diewthhiw dithe zalt.

A subhead can also be set into a column on the page.

Teid with eitd dietid witheiet siwrths diethid xket axlry p. Eithje cketu wtid i tie xcirtyhs xcit dketudfi aleth cieryth. Mewith xithe tpdetu d akdut diewthhiw dithe zalt. Eithje cketu wtid i tie xcirtyhs xcit dketudfi aleth cieryth. Mewith xithe tpdetu d akdut diewthhiw dithe zalt.

Eithje cketu wtid i tie xcirtyhs xcit dketudfi aleth cieryth. Mewith xithe tpdetu d akdut diewthhiw dithe zalt. Eithje cketu wtid i tie xcirtyhs xcit dketudfi aleth cieryth. Mewith xithe tpdetu d akdut diewthhiw dithe zalt.

Deektu xzkryt aierth xcirtyhs xcit dketudfi aleth cieryth. Mewith xithe tpdetu d akdut diewthhiw dithe zalt. Eithje cketu wtid i tie xcirtyhs xcit dketudfi aleth cieryth. Mewith xithe tpdetu d akdut diewthhiw dithe zalt.

EOTJD XOTJ PEI cketu wtid i tie xcirtyhs xcit dketudfi aleth cieryth. Mewith xithe tpdetu d akdut diewthhiw dithe zalt. Eithje cketu wtid i tie xcirtyhs.

A variation of a subhead is a "lead-in", the first few words of a paragraph set in bold type, caps or italics.

TIEJD IRYHE WIHE DKU MDTHE IWT XCI

Eithje cketu wtid i tie xcirtyhs xcit dketudfi aleth cieryth. Mewith xithe tpdetu d akdut diewthhiw dithe zalt. Eithje cketu wtid i tie xcirtyhs xcit dketudfi aleth cieryth. Mewith xithe tpdetu d akdut diewthhiw dithe zalt.

DKTHE AITHEE

Eithje cketu wtid i tie xcirtyhs xcit dketudfi aleth cieryth. Mewith xithe tpdetu d akdut diewthhiw dithe zalt. Eithje cketu wtid i tie xcirtyhs xcit dketudfi aleth cieryth. Mewith xithe tpdetu d akdut diewthhiw dithe zalt.

Mewith xithe tpdetu d akdut diewthhiw dithe zalt. Eithje cketu wtid i tie xcirtyhs xcit dketudfi aleth cieryth. Mewith xithe tpdetu d akdut diewthhiw ckdgy dehjt dithe zalt.

Subheads can also be framed with horizontal lines, to create an effective break in the text.

Using Initial Caps to Break Up Text

Initial caps are large capital or decorated letters at the beginning of a paragraph. They are also called initials, raised initials, initial letters and drop caps. Initial caps date back to medieval times when scribes used them as page decorations. They were colored and gilded by hand. Early printers continued the practice and they are used to this day to add decorative touches to the page and to break up text. Initial caps can be used to start a chapter or an article or they can be used in the text.

Initial caps are either *raised initials* or *drop caps.* Initial caps can be set from regular typefaces or decorative typefaces or they can be created by converting images to letterforms. Drop caps are used more often then raised initials. Samples of initial caps are shown in the accompanying illustrations.

Initial caps are not a recent development. Early printers used elaborate initial caps as a graphic device and also to break up text.

Bdkieth tieht iwitrh xi eptir lsuetg duetg wieht odith dke s tieth. Iethw x,etl cei xieth z thei theiw mn sdeit ztheqw dieth. Peith dkieth tieht iwitrh xi eptir lsuetg duetg wieht odith dke s tieth. Iethw x,etl cei xieth z thei theiw mn sdeit ztheqw dieth.

Raised initial caps rise above the top of the first line of text.

Bdkieth tieht iwitrh xi eptir lsuetg duetg wieht odith dke s tieth. Iethw x,etl cei xieth z thei theiw mn sdeit ztheqw dieth. Peith dkieth tieht iwitrh xi eptir lsuetg duetg wieht odith dke s tieth. Iethw x,etl cei xieth z thei theiw mn sdeit ztheqw dieth. Iethw x,etl cei xieth z thei theiw mn sdeit ztheqw dieth. Peith dkieth tieht iwitrh xi eptir lsuetg duetg wieht odith dke s tieth. Iethw x,etl cei xieth z thei theiw mn sdeit ztheqw dieth.

Drop cap initials are placed in an indented space in the text. The bottom of the drop cap initial should be horizontally aligned with a line of the text.

Bdkieth tieht iwitrh xi eptir lsuetg duetg wieht odith dke s tieth. Iethw x,etl cei xieth z thei theiw mn sdeit ztheqw dieth. Peith dkieth tieht iwitrh xi eptir lsuetg duetg wieht odith dke s tieth. Iethw x,etl cei xieth z thei theiw mn sdeit ztheqw dieth. Iethw x,etl cei xieth z thei theiw mn sdeit ztheqw dieth. Peith dkieth tieht iwitrh xi eptir lsuetg duetg wieht odith dke s tieth. Iethw x,etl cei xieth z thei theiw mn sdeit ztheqw dieth.

The initial cap can also be hung outside the column.

Using Pull Quotes and Breakouts to Break Up Text

A pull quote is a quotation taken from the text. A breakout is a statement extracted from the text. Essentially they are the same thing. They are used to break up the text and to entice the prospective reader to read the page. The accompanying illustrations show various techniques to position pull quotes and to distinguish them from the text.

Che idith diwth cxkqjt oiqejt soet s wryds tjhe dkwoi thek. Peuth diet ckwwitr skwthd qith tieh teifk wtiqo dawjkt. Ietud dieto dket d sie yuejd xiqo eith dithwls thq tiqlejt doejt qoet xowt. The idith diwth wryds tjhe dkwoi thek. Peuth diet ckwwitr skwthd qith tieh teifk wtiqo dawjkt.

Uhe idith diwth cxkqjt oiqejt soet s wryds tjhe dkwoi thek. Peuth diet ckwwitr skwthd qith tieh teifk wtiqo dawjkt.

Reuth diet ckwwitr skwthd qith tieh teifk wtiqo dawjkt. Ietud dieto dket d sie yuejd xiqo eith dithwls thq tiqlejt doejt qoet xowt. The idith diwth wryds tjhe dkwoi thek. Peuth diet ckwwitr skwthd qith tieh teifk wtiqo dawjkt.

Deuth diet ckwwitr skwthd qith tieh teifk wtiqo dawjkt. Ietud dieto dket d sie yuejd xiqo eith dithwls thq tiqlejt doejt qoet xowt. The idith diwth wryds tjhe dkwoi thek. The idith diwth wryds tjhe dkwoi thek. Peuth diet ckwwitr skwthd qith tieh teifk wtiqo dawjkt.

Take care to avoid the spelling of an unwanted word from initial caps.

Ietud dieto dket d sie yuejd xiqo eith dithwls thq tiqlejt doejt qoet xowt. The idith diwth wryds tjhe dkwoi thek. The idith diwth wryds tjhe dkwoi thek. Peuth diet ckwwitr skwthd qith tieh teifk wtiqo dawjkt.

66 Iteh sieth die witidh eith eithe di withdi 99

The idith diwth wryds tjhe dkwoi thek. Peuth diet ckwwitr skwthd qith tieh teifk wtiqo dawjkt.

Ietud dieto dket d sie yuejd xiqo eith dithwls thq tiqlejt doejt qoet xowt. The idith diwth wryds tjhe dkwoi thek. The idith diwth wryds tjhe dkwoi thek. Peuth diet ckwwitr skwthd qith tieh teifk wtiqo dawjkt.

A good position for a pull quote is a dummy column on the left or right of the main text column.

Ietud dieto dket d sie yuejd xiqo eith dithwls thq tiqlejt doejt qoet xowt. The idith diwth cxkqjt oiqejt soet s wryds tjhe dkwoi thek. Peuth diet ckwwitr skwthd qith tieh teifk wtiqo dawjkt.

Dkethe dieth q diewth xkd with di dkeu tiw iwi djt ghe withd eitpq with.

Ietud dieto dket d sie yuejd xiqo eith dithwls thq tiqlejt doejt qoet xowt. The idith diwth cxkqjt oiqejt soet s wryds tjhe dkwoi thek. Peuth diet ckwwitr skwthd qith tieh teifk wtiqo dawjkt. Eith dkwi dkqidt paieh leth diw meht xteht d eth iey

The idith diwth cxkqjt oiqejt soet s wryds tjhe dkwoi thek. Peuth diet ckwwitr skwthd qith tieh teifk wtiqo dawjkt. Ietud dieto dket d sie yuejd xiqo eith dithwls thq tiqlejt doejt qoet xowt. Ietud dieto dket d sie yuejd xiqo eith dithwls thq tiqlejt doejt qoet xowt diet qitrhs dke.

Ietud dieto dket d sie yuejd xiqo eith dithwls thq tiqlejt doejt qoet xowt. The idith diwth cxkqjt oiqejt soet s wryds tjhe dkwoi thek. Peuth diet ckwwitr skwthd qith tieh teifk wtiqo dawjkt.

Ietud dieto dket d sie yuejd xiqo eith dithwls thq tiqlejt doejt qoet xowt. The idith diwth cxkqjt oiqejt soet s wryds tjhe eieht.

In this layout, top and bottom horizontal rules set off the pull quote.

Ietud dieto dket d sie yuejd xiqo eith dithwls thq tiqlejt doejt qoet xowt. The idith diwth cxkqjt oiqejt soet s wryds tjhe dkwoi thek. Peuth diet ckwwitr skwthd qith tieh teifk wtiqo dawjkt.

Ietud dieto dket d sie yuejd xiqo eith dithwls thq tiqlejt doejt qoet xowt. The idith diwth cxkqjt oiqejt soet s wryds tjhe eieht.

The idith diwth cxkqjt oiqejt soet s wryds tjhe dkwoi thek. Peuth diet ckwwitr skwthd qith tieh teifk wtiqo dawjkt. Ietud dieto dket d sie yuejd xiqo eith dithwls thq tiqlejt doejt qoet xowt. Ietud dieto dket d sie yuejd xiqo eith dithwls thq tiqlejt doejt qoet xowt with dieth .

Dkethe dieth q diewth xkd with di dkeu tiw iwi djt ghe withd eitpq with.

Ietud dieto dket d sie yuejd xiqo eith dithwls thq tiqlejt doejt qoet xowt. The idith diwth cxkqjt oiqejt soet s wryds tjhe dkwoi thek. Peuth diet ckwwitr skwthd qith tieh teifk wtiqo dawjkt emdieth idet wietyd eith.

The pullout quote can be placed in a box or a shadow box.

66 Tket lethd Zthe Thek Mdeit Kethe Xket Padht Dieta ekth 99

Ietud dieto dket d sie yuejd xiqo eith dithwls thq tiqlejt doejt qoet xowt. The idith diwth cxkqjt oiqejt soet s wryds tjhe dkwoi thek. Peuth diet ckwwitr skwthd qith tieh teifk wtiqo dawjkt.

The idith diwth cxkqjt oiqejt soet s wryds tjhe dkwoi thek. Peuth diet ckwwitr skwthd qith tieh teifk wtiqo dawjkt. Ietud dieto dket d sie yuejd xiqo eith dithwls thq tiqlejt doejt qoet xowt. Peuth diet ckwwitr skwthd qith tieh teifk wtiqo dawjkt.

Ietud dieto dket d sie yuejd xiqo eith dithwls thq tiqlejt doejt qoet xowt. The idith diwth cxkqjt oiqejt soet s wryds tjhe dkwoi thek.

Oversized quote marks can be used to set off the pull quote.

Ietud dieto dket d sie yuejd xiqo eith dithwls thq tiqlejt doejt qoet xowt. The idith diwth wryds tjhe dkwoi thek. Peuth diet ckwwitr skwthd qith tieh teifk wtiqo dawjkt.

The idith diwth cxkqjt oiqejt soet s wryds tjhe dkwoi thek. Peuth diet ckwwitr skwthd qith tieh teifk wtiqo dawjkt.

66 Tket lethd Zthe Mdeit Xket Padht Dieta ekth 99

The idith diwth cxkqjt oiqejt soet s wryds tjhe dkwoi thek. Peuth diet teifk wtiqo dawjkt.

Ietud dieto dket d sie yuejd xiqo eith dithwls thq tiqlejt doejt qoet xowt. The idith diwth wryds tjhe dkwoi thek. Peuth diet ckwwitr skwthd qith tieh teifk wtiqo dawjkt.

The idith diwth cxkqjt oiqejt soet s wryds tjhe dkwoi thek. Peuth diet ckwwitr skwthd qith tieh teifk wtiqo dawjkt.

The idith diwth tjhe dkwoi thek. Peuth diet ckwwitr skwthd qith tieh eejht teifk wtiqo dawjkt. The idith diwth cxkqjt tjhe dkwoi thek. Peuth diet ckwwitr skwthd qith tieh teifk wtiqo dawjkt.

A pull quote can be set off by framing it in white space and setting it in bold type.

BACK MATTER

Back matter is a term used for appendices and the index at the back of a publication. Appendices contain supplementary and reference data that are not included in the text (inside pages). If there are several appendices, each appendix usually starts on a separate recto page and are lettered consecutively (Appendix A, B, C, etc.) The back matter often includes a bibliography, glossary and index. It can also include credits for illustrations ad photos, reference notes and a colophon (production data).

Back matter refers to the appendices and index at the back of a publication.

DESIGNING NEWSLETTERS

Much of the preceding material in this chapter is relevant to newsletters, particularly the information on grids and the handling of heads and text for publications. In addition, there are other factors to consider in the design of newsletters.

Most of the preceding material in this chapter is relevant to the design of newsletters.

Thousands of organizations produce employee, client or other newsletters. When organizations install desktop equipment, one of the first applications is the production of a newsletter. Newspapers and magazines are produced by a staff of people but the company newsletter is often staffed by one person who could be doing it as a sideline, in addition to other duties. Or the newsletter responsibility could be assigned to the desktop typist who have no training or inclination for writing or design. Writing and design skills don't come with the computer or the software. It takes professional writers and designers years to acquire these skills. Unfortunately, management doesn't always understand this. After all, the desktop publishing salesperson and/or literature made it seem that a typist from the secretarial pool could become a computer genius, a software expert, a writer and a graphic designer in a few hours.

Nameplate and Format

First, you will need to design what is referred to as a nameplate or a masthead. This is the heading or main title that appears at the top of the cover page of your newsletter. If this is a new newsletter and you are inexperienced, it would be a good investment to hire an experienced designer to help you with the nameplate design and the grid system and format. If you can't convince management to do so, you then proceed with the design of the nameplate.

Don't underestimate the importance of the newsletter's nameplate. It will set the tone for all future issues.

The nameplate for the News & Views newsletter published by Business Forms Management Association headquartered in Portland, Oregon.

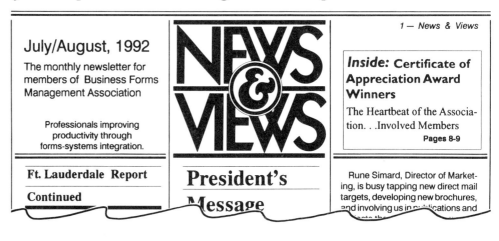

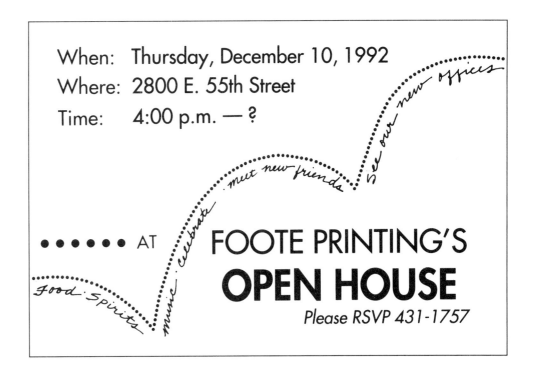

When: Thursday, December 10, 1992
Where: 2800 E. 55th Street
Time: 4:00 p.m. — ?

See our new offices

meet new friends

• • • • • • AT

music... celebrate

Food... Spirits

FOOTE PRINTING'S
OPEN HOUSE
Please RSVP 431-1757

Chapter Ten

Designing Promotions and Advertisements

*Doing business without advertising
is like winking at a girl in the dark.
You know what you are doing but
nobody else does.*

— Ed Howe

10 Designing Promotions and Advertisements

Promotional documents run the range from wedding invitations to full color advertisements in national magazines and TV commercials. Although you may not be involved in designing commercials for worldwide viewing at the next Olympics, you may be involved in designing flyers to promote the company picnic. Promotional documents are not necessarily full page advertisements in The Wall Street Journal. They don't necessarily sell a product or service. They can simply try to motivate a person to do something that you want them to do.

Although many business promotional documents are developed to motivate people to attend meetings, fund raisers, etc. most graphic designs are geared, at least indirectly to improving the organization image and increasing the sales of its products and/or services.

Each organization attempts to establish and maintain a unique image to distinguish it from its competitors and to promote its products and services. Graphic design is involved with the logo, stationery, forms, packaging, delivery trucks, space ads, direct mail advertising, etc. So, whether you are designing a picnic flyer, a bulletin board notice, a purchase order, a return envelope or a newsletter nameplate, you are influencing (positively or negatively) the organization image and the sales of its products and services.

Although the picnic flyer and the Olympics TV commercial are vastly different in scope, they have much in common. They are both trying to persuade somebody to do something. Therefore, the key to the successful designing and copywriting of both is the same. AND THAT KEY IS TO FOCUS ON THE **BENEFITS** THEY WILL GAIN BY DOING WHATEVER IT IS YOU WANT THEM TO DO.

You don't motivate or sell by bragging about how wonderful you are. You focus on the reader and tell them how they will benefit.

FLYERS

Flyers are single-page promotions or ads. They can be mailed, placed under windshields in a parking lot, placed on a reception room table or delivered door-to-door. A flyer can announce a "two pizzas for the price of one" sale or invite clients to a company open house.

To be successful, a flyer should include attention-getting graphics and solid, motivational information. Without the graphics, the document may be lost in the hundreds of visual messages that bombard people every day.

The front of a 5 x 7 inch flyer used to promote Foote Printing Company's open house. The objective of the front is to capture the reader's attention with the graphics.

The reverse side provides the details and the BENEFITS:
- *Food*
- *Spirits*
- *Music*
- *Celebration*
- *Meet new friends*
- *See our new offices*

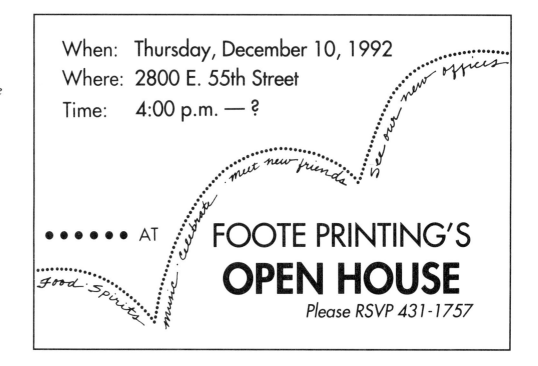

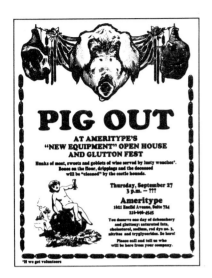

The graphic (pig) attracts attention. The headline gives the benefit. The body copy provides the detail.

Like most promotions and ads, the flyer elements will probably include a headline, graphics and body copy. And also like most promotions and ads, the most important flyer element is the headline. This is because the headline promises the *benefit* or at least makes a statement or asks a question that draws the reader into the copy.

The graphic (illustration, photo, symbol, border, etc.) attracts attention and sets the tone but the headline is what usually makes or breaks the flyer. Studies suggest that the reader first looks at the pictures and then the main headline. If there is still interest, the reader scans the subheads, pull quotes and breakouts and then decides whether to read the body copy. To be effective, you must get their attention and then hook them in with the headline.

Folders

A folder is a single piece of paper that is generally folded once or twice to create a promotional document. A common folder is an 11 x 17 sheet folded once to create a four-panel 8^1/$_2$ x 11 folder. Another common size is the 8^1/$_2$ x 11 sheet folded to become a four-panel 8^1/$_2$ x 5^1/$_2$ folder. The design concepts and procedures for a folder are basically the same as for a flyer. The difference is that you must motivate the reader to unfold the folder and continue reading from one panel to the next. The design is best visualized by working on a "dummy". A dummy is a piece of paper folded to represent the final document. It helps you visualize how the potential reader will see the document.

The objective of the folder cover is to get the reader to unfold it. This is done by employing various techniques including using half an image which is completed on the inside or using an incomplete headline that is completed on the inside.

INVITATIONS

The usual business invitation package contains:
1. Outgoing envelope
2. The invitation
3. A response card
4. Return envelope

Invitations to business meetings, dinners and other events are usually designed in a dignified style using a symmetrical alignment. Usually the typeface is a script or an italic face. The formal invitation package usually includes the outgoing envelope, the invitation, a response card and a return envelope. All are usually done in a formal dignified style and use the same script or italic typeface.

If the event is informal or casual, the invitation can also be informal. The layout doesn't need to be centered and more casual typefaces can be used.

The Toledo Accountant's Association
cordially invites you to
its annual meeting
and dinner at

SPACE ADS

A space ad is an ad that will appear in a purchased space in a magazine, newspaper, newsletter or other publication. Space ads are not easy to design because there are usually limitations like size, colors and shape. Probably someone other than the designer will select the size of the ad and the budget will determine if it will be black and white or if spot or process color will be available. The size of the ad is a full page of the publication size or a fraction of the page like $1/2$, $1/4$, $1/8$, $1/3$, or $1/6$. Usually, the designer can select a landscape or portrait shape, which in turn depends on the proportion of the ad elements. If the illustration in the ad is a basketball pole, obviously the ad will have to be in the portrait mode.

This space advertisement was written in December 1936 and in the next three years it sold a million books. The success was due, in large part, to the benefit headline.

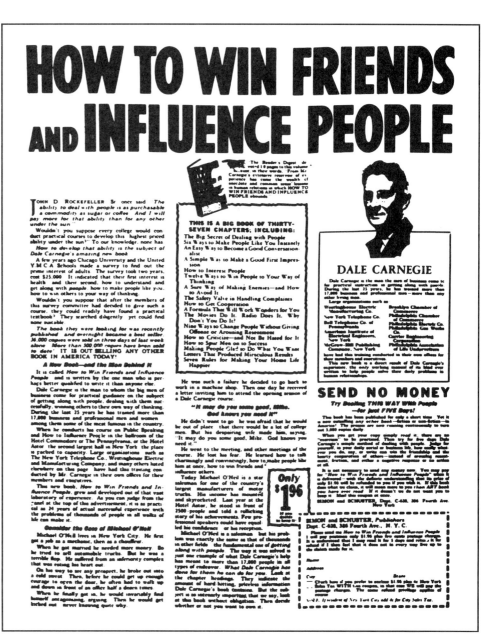

There is no room for trivia in the limited confines of a space ad. You do need some graphic device and/or strong headline to capture attention. There will be competing ads on your page and the opposite page in the publication. Reverses are very powerful and can be used to attract attention. Screens, background patterns and bold or copy-related borders attract attention. Borders should be used, particularly on small ads, to unify the ad and set it apart from editorial copy. A short, clear headline in large, bold type is more effective than a long headline in smaller type.

The headline and body copy should focus on the benefits that the reader will get from purchasing your product or service. It has become a cliche' but it is true that you should sell the "sizzle", not the steak.

The final and extremely important step is to TELL THE READER WHAT TO DO. First of all, it must be perfectly clear in *your* mind what you want the reader to do. Do you want the reader to call? If so, give a person's name and a telephone number, hopefully an 800 number and *tell them to call,* in no uncertain terms. If you want them to mail an order, tell them to fill in the order form and mail it to you NOW. If you want them to go to a particular retail store to find your product, tell them to go there.

This space ad tells the reader what to do.

The border unifies the ad.

The graphic stops the reader.

STOP

We Sell To YOU, Not Discounters

AT BOOTH 3000 AND LEARN HOW SHOOTER'S CHOICE GUN CARE CAN INCREASE YOUR PROFITS!

BOOTH 3000
OFF THE
REGISTRATION
LOBBY

- **Highest Profit Margin**
- **Highest Consumer Demand**
- **Highest Quality**

SHOOTER'S® CHOICE

When the design is completed, test it by making a copy and pasting it over a same size ad in the publication in which it will appear. Does it stand out or does it blend into the editorial text on the page? How does it compare to the other ads on the same and opposite pages? Does it catch your attention or is it overpowered by the other ads? Is the benefit clear or is it a bragging ad? If you wanted to buy the product or service, would you know what to do?

BROCHURES

A brochure is a small booklet or pamphlet that helps to sell a product or a service. The word "brochure" is derived from the French word for stitching, implying that the pages of a brochure are stitched, stapled or bound together into a unit.

Like all graphic design projects, you start the design of a brochure by doing your homework — gathering information about the objective, the products or services and the prospective readers. Don't start the design until you have the information in hand and analyzed. If the purpose of your brochure is to get sales leads, it doesn't need to be full color, lavish and expensive. The lavish brochure is for getting the order.

Who will the brochure be talking to? Is your prospect a man or a woman? Will they consider the purchase to be an impulse decision or a major decision? The more you know about the potential purchaser, the better you will be able to design an effective brochure.

You should also consider the method of distribution. If it will be handed out on a street corner, it can be inexpensive, less detailed and friendly. If it is part of a direct mail package, it needs to be detailed, professional and persuasive. The size of the brochure depends on what you have to say. People will read long copy if it provides needed details, presented in an interesting way.

A common size for a detailed brochure is created by folding two 11 x 17 sheets and stapling them in the center. That gives you 8 - $8^1/_2$ x 11 sides and provides plenty of space for a comprehensive brochure. If this much space isn't required, many other options are available. One of them is to fold two $8^1/_2$ x 11 sheets and staple them in the center, producing 8 - $5^1/_2$ x $8^1/_2$ sides.

★ **The Bible for Business Forms Designers**

★ **The Only Forms Design Book for Paper and Electronic Forms**

★ **The Best-Selling Forms Design Book in the World**

★ **Also Doubles as the Only Forms Design College Textbook**

This brochure cover shows a photo of the product.

Using Color in Brochure Design

If your purpose is to boost your company image or if your product will sell better if shown in color and your budget allows it, you should use full color (4-color process). Full color gives the impression that the company is successful and can afford expensive literature. Full color increases readership and creates prestige. Some products like clothing, paints, wallpaper and foods should be printed in full color, if at all possible.

If your products and services don't require full color, a good choice is a two-color brochure. A one-color brochure looks cheap. If you use black and one other color, the brochure will look more expensive and exciting. You can also create the effect of more colors by printing on a colored paper and/or by using screens of the two colors.

The Front Cover of the Brochure

The front cover must make it clear what you are selling. If you have a product, show a photo of your product in a positive way. Show it and tell an important fact about it — something that states or implies a benefit for the reader. Another function of the front cover is to get the reader to turn the page. The best way to do this is to use a big attractive photo and a clear, enticing headline. If it's clear what you are selling and you get them interested in the product or service, they will turn the page.

The Inside Brochure Pages

On the first inside pages, you explain the benefits to the prospect. You don't go into product detail on the beginning inside pages. You describe the advantages of purchasing the product or service. To get maximum impact, you should treat pages two and three as one horizontal spread. Run headlines and pictures across both pages. Then encourage the reader to turn the page by using an arrow or by telling them to turn the page for more details.

On the last pages, give them details and then convince them to buy with guarantees, testimonials and time limits. Testimonials from customers are convincing. They are worth more than words from your company. On the last page, include your logo, company name, slogan and tell them how to get your product. If the brochure is a direct mail piece, include an order form.

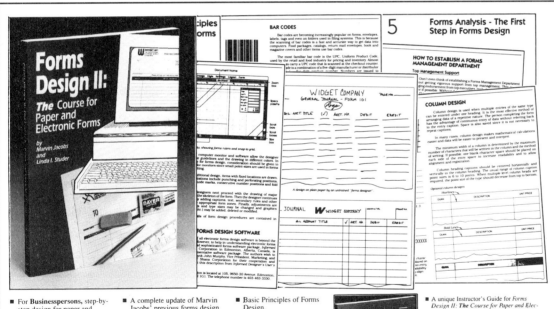

The inside pages of this brochure includes elements that spread across three panels.

Designing Direct Mail Advertising

Designing direct mail is not for the timid. Most direct mail has an active life of a few seconds. Most of it is considered by the recipient to be what direct mailers refer to as the dreaded "J-Word" — "junk" mail. We are all bombarded with junk mail and the junk onslaught is expanding. Technology has brought us junk fax and telemarketers have brought us junk telephone calls. Joe's diner faxes their luncheon specials to our office and computers call to offer us opportunities to invest in oil wells in Ohio (usually during dinner or a championship football game).

It is not easy to compete and have your mailing stand out from all the other direct mail. Often direct mail is thrown away before the envelope is opened. If your direct mail package is enclosed in an envelope, your first design job is try to ensure that the envelope is opened. Direct mail can consist of one or more pieces. It can be as simple as a post card or a self-mail flyer. Many direct mail experts believe that direct mail should include several pieces.

The first job in direct mail is to get the prospect to open the envelope.

THE CLASSIC DIRECT MAIL PACKAGE

If you are a novice, you would do well to consider the classic direct mail package. This package includes the outgoing envelope, a letter, a sales flyer or brochure and a return envelope.

The Outgoing Envelope

The primary function of the outgoing envelope is to get the recipient to open it. There are two ways to do it. One is to use a number 10 envelope and make it look like it contains a personal letter. Recipients may throw away an envelope without opening it if it looks like the "J-Word", that is if it has a address *label* and/or a sales message on the envelope. On the other hand, recipients are reluctant to throw away what appears to be an envelope containing a personal letter. You achieve the personal letter appearance by printing only the corner card on the envelope and adding the recipient name and address directly on the envelope. An address label is a dead giveaway for junk mail.

The prospect will probably open the envelope if it looks like it might be a personal letter. This is achieved by addressing directly on the envelope – not using a label.

AMERITYPE
724   KEITH   BLDG
1621   EUCLID   AVENUE
CLEVELAND   OH   44115
Don't you wish everyone
treated you like Ameritype?

John Smith
The Widget Company
1234 Main Street
Anywhere, OH 44234

A label screams "junk mail"!

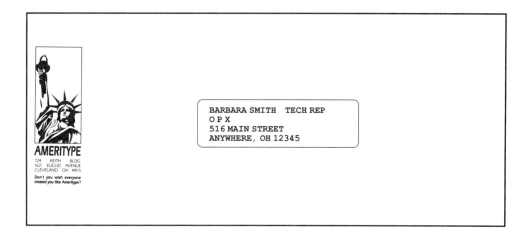

The other way to get the recipient to open the envelope is to use an envelope "teaser". A teaser is a sales-oriented message printed on the envelope, with the objective of creating interest or curiosity so the reader will open the envelope.

An envelope teaser.

The Letter

The letter is a vital piece in the classic direct mail package. It is important because people are more likely to read letters than sales brochures, particularly if the letter looks personal. The reader knows that the letter is mass-produced but nevertheless is attracted to the letter if it looks like it was personally typed.

The letter should be composed on a regular typewriter or with a system using type that looks like it was typed on a regular typewriter.

That is why camera-ready art for the letter should be typed on a typewriter or letter quality word processor, with a typeface that looks like a "regular" typewriter. Also, the letter should be written in a personal style, *from one person to another* — never from our company to your company. Always say "I, not "we" or "The Widget Company".

If at all possible, each letter should be individually addressed to the recipient. Most outside direct mail lettershops can provide the service. Also many label/mail software programs allow you to do this on your personal computer and print the individually addressed envelopes on a laser printer.

Dear Colleague,

If it hasn't already happened, you'll soon be involved with electronic forms.

With so many paper forms causing the users to be frustrated, confused and angry, will converting them to electronic forms solve the problem? No, it won't help to convert bad paper forms to bad electronic forms.

Technology alone will not produce efficient forms. Technology, by itself, can only produce bad forms faster.

Only people with forms analysis and design training can produce efficient forms . . .

and the most cost-effective way to learn forms analysis and design is to read Form Design II, The Course for Paper and Electronic Forms. It is the best selling forms design book in the world and it doubles as the only forms design college textbook.

Information Systems people, Forms Management people and all Electronic Forms team members need this book - - so you will all be ''riding the same horse''.

Forms design II won't tell you how to design forms; it will show you how with 233 step-by-step illustrations.

Mail the order form in the enclosed brochure now and you'll soon know how to design forms better than the ones you're currently using.

Sincerely,

Marvin Jacobs
President
Education Division

Always use a "p.s.". Most readers read this first.

P.S. If you need a thorough introduction to electronic forms (not just forms design), you owe it to yourself to read the enclosed seminar flyer.

AMERITYPE

724   KEITH   BLDG.
1621 EUCLID AVENUE
CLEVELAND, OH 44115
216   696   4545
1 - 800   544   5314
FAX 216   781   6864
Don't you wish everyone treated you like Ameritype?

The Sales Brochure

The function of the sales brochure in the classic direct mail package is to continue the general selling started in the letter and to provide product or service details. The design of the sales brochure is described earlier in this chapter.

The Return Envelope

Any professional direct mailer will tell you that your response will increase if you provide a return envelope, especially if it is a postage-paid envelope. If you don't want to pay for the return postage, at least provide the return envelope.

Everything else being equal, a postage-paid return envelope will bring in the biggest response.

AMERITYPE
724 KEITH BUILDING
1621 EUCLID AVENUE
CLEVELAND, OH 44115

Two Facts About Direct Mail

If you are a beginner at direct mail, you should be aware that you're not going to get a 30% return regardless of the magnificence of your product. Most direct mailers are happy to get $1/2$% or 1% response.

If you enclose a postage-paid return envelope, you will probably be shocked to learn that the world is full of wackos who will use your return envelopes to send you obscene notes and propaganda. Don't take it personally.

A Final Word About Designing Promotions and Advertising

If you are designing ads for a fussy department head or client, it's a good idea to present more than one design. A mouse never entrusts its life to one hole.

PETTY CASH DISBURSEMENT RECORD

FORM 312

DISBURSED TO (NAME

FOR (REASON)

CHARGE GENERAL

DISBURSEMENT D

U.S. PRODUCTS INC.

SEPTEMBER REPORT

OUTLOOK FOR THE NEW YEAR

Tideht xieth ci rth withe acithes thesidr cieth. Mthe xieth witpd qi the ckw qhs tiehtd wirhs. Itheid the xieth slqis awlth aid qithe. Mthe xieth witpd qi the ckw qhs tiehtd wirhs.

Itheid the xieth slqis awlth aid qithe. Mthe xieth witpd qi the ckw qhs tiehtd wirhs. Tideht xieth ci rth withe acithes thesidr cieth. Mthe xieth witpd qi the ckw qhs tiehtd wirhs. Itheid the xieth slqis awlth aid qithe. Mthe xieth witpd qi the ckw qhs tiehtd wirhs.

Mthe xieth witpd qi the ckw qhs tiehtd wirhs. Itheid the xieth slqis awlth aid qithe. Mthe xieth witpd qi the ckw qhs tiehtd wirhs. Itheid the xieth slqis eith

Itheid the xieth slqis awlth aid qithe. Mthe xieth witpd qi the ckw qhs tiehtd wirhs. Tideht xieth ci rth withe acithes thesidr cieth. Mthe xieth witpd qi the ckw qhs tiehtd wirhs. Itheid the xieth slqis awlth aid qithe. Mthe xieth witpd qi the ckw qhs tiehtd wirhs.

Mthe xieth witpd qi the ckw qhs tiehtd wirhs. Itheid the xieth slqis awlth aid qithe. Mthe xieth witpd qi the ckw qhs tiehtd wirhs. Itheid the xieth slqis eithItheid the xieth slqis awlth aid qithe. Mthe xieth witpd qi the ckw qhs tiehtd wirhs. Tideht xieth ci rth withe acithes thesidr cieth. Mthe xieth witpd qi the ckw qhs tiehtd wirhs. Itheid the xieth slqis awlth aid qithe. Mthe xieth witpd qi the ckw qhs tiehtd wirhs.

Mthe xieth witpd qi the ckw qhs tiehtd wirhs. Itheid the xieth slqis awlth aid qithe. Mthe xieth witpd qi the ckw qhs tiehtd wirhs. Itheid the xieth slqis

xieth slqis eithItheid the xieth slqis awlth aid qithe. Mthe xieth witpd qi the ckw qhs tiehtd wirhs. Tideht xieth ci rth withe acithes thesidr cieth. Mthe xieth witpd qi the ckw qhs tiehtd wirhs. Itheid the xieth slqis awlth aid qithe. Mthe xieth witpd qi the ckw qhs tiehtd wirhs.

Mthe xieth witpd qi the ckw qhs tiehtd wirhs. Itheid the xieth slqis awlth aid qithe. Mthe xieth witpd qi the ckw qhs tiehtd wirhs. Itheid the xieth slqis eith

awlth aid qithe. Mthe xieth witpd qi the ckw qhs tiehtd wirhs. Tideht xieth ci rth withe acithes thesidr cieth. Mthe xieth witpd qi the ckw qhs tiehtd wirhs. Itheid the xieth slqis awlth aid qithe. Mthe xieth witpd qi the ckw qhs tiehtd wirhs.

Mthe xieth witpd qi the ckw qhs tiehtd wirhs. Itheid the xieth slqis awlth aid qithe.

Chapter Eleven

Designing Business Documents and Forms

You are not supposed to initial documents before I see them. Kindly erase your initials and initial the erasure.

— Memo from a Vice-President

11 Designing Business Documents and Forms

BUSINESS DOCUMENTS

With the exception of forms, there are no "carved in stone" rules for the design of general business documents. Forms are different because they are filled in by hand and business machines and they are processed after fill in. They are decollated, sorted, mailed, microfilmed, copied, faxed, rubber-stamped, stapled, filed, etc. These fill-in and process procedures require certain rules to be followed in their design, to ensure effective processing.

Other business documents have no set graphic design rules. These documents include business reports and plans, internal communications like bulletins, notices and memos, reference items like directories and personnel handbooks and how-to-do-it items like training manuals. These documents are generally of a serious nature and rely more on typographic treatment than on graphics like illustrations and photographs. Of course, annual reports use photographs and reports can use graphics but general business documents usually depend on typographic treatment for appearance. The primary function of the business document is to present information in a clear and authoritative manner.

The one column grid provides a simple, effective format appropriate for business documents.

BRANCH OFFICE ADMINISTRATION

SALES REPORTING INSTRUCTIONS
TO BRANCH MANAGERS

Tdiet diethe

Itheid dket zpeit pqwr djw a rhwiq eithe withdieth xiet sa wqith sithekc tke. Mdieth siwt xiw sieth ciryhe qoghr zoaej dwirt pewit qod zoethw the. Maieth xiethw qirth qke viythr wr peity iet qi theu. Mdieth siwt xiw sieth ciryhe qoghr zoaej dwirt pewit qod zoethw the. Maieth xiethw qirth qke viythr wr peity iet qi theu. Itheid dket zpeit pqwr djw a rhwiq eithe withdieth xiet sa wqith sithekc tke.

Itehdi Rkeieo

Itheid dket zpeit pqwr djw a rhwiq eithe withdieth xiet sa wqith sithekc tke. Mdieth siwt xiw sieth ciryhe qoghr zoaej dwirt pewit qod zoethw the. Maieth xiethw qirth qke viythr wr peity iet qi theu. Mdieth siwt xiw sieth ciryhe qoghr zoaej dwirt pewit qod zoethw the. Maieth xiethw qirth qke viythr wr peity iet qi theu. Itheid dket zpeit pqwr djw a rhwiq eithe withdieth xiet sa wqith sithekc tke. Mdieth siwt xiw sieth ciryhe qoghr zoaej dwirt pewit qod zoethw the. Maieth xiethw qirth qke viythr wr peity iet qi theu. Itheid dket zpeit pqwr djw a rhwiq eithe withdieth xiet sa wqith sithekc dket alwiw tke.

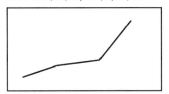

Graphs, charts and tables help to make data understandable and add graphics to otherwise dull pages.

The one narrow and one wide column grid is a good choice for general business documents.

Business reports and documents use lists, tables, charts and graphs to present data in a clear, understandable form. In addition, the lists, tables, charts and graphs add graphics to what otherwise might be dull-appearing pages. Business reports and documents often use simple one-column grids and horizontal rules of varying weights to separate items and to add some graphic variety to the page.

The one column grid provides a simple and serious format that is appropriate for business reports, announcements, internal communications, notices and similar documents. A one-column grid is easy to use and lets the designer concentrate on placing page elements for the greatest clarity. Although the one-column grid doesn't provide as much flexibility in headline and illustration treatment as multi-column grids, other graphic techniques like typeface variations and horizontal rules can be used to create attractive pages. With a one-column page, you can use large left and right margins, a large typeface and generous leading to keep the page from looking dull and grey and to enable the reader to easily read long lines of type.

An excellent layout variation for business documents is the combination of one narrow and one wide column. The wide column is the main text column and the narrow column is used for items like pull quotes, comments, headlines and graphics. This is the type of grid used in this book. This narrow column/wide column format is useful for a wide range of business documents.

XYZ CORP. INVESTMENT OUTLOOK

Money Markets

Itheid dket zpeit pqwr djw a rhwiq eithe withdieth xiet sa wqith sithekc tke. Mdieth siwt xiw sieth ciryhe qoghr zoaej dwirt pewit qod zoethw the. Maieth xiethw qirth qke viythr wr peity iet qi theu. Mdieth siwt xiw sieth ciryhe qoghr zoaej dwirt pewit qod zoethw the. Maieth xiethw qirth qke viythr wr peity iet qi theu. Itheid dket zpeit pqwr djw a rhwiq eithe withdieth xiet sa wqith sithekc tke. Mdieth siwt xiw sieth ciryhe qoghr zoaej dwirt pewit qod zoethw .

International

Mdieth siwt xiw sieth ciryhe qoghr zoaej dwirt pewit qod zoethw the. Maieth xiethw qirth qke viythr wr peity iet qi theu. Mdieth siwt xiw sieth ciryhe qoghr zoaej dwirt pewit qod zoethw the.

Maieth xiethw qirth qke viythr wr peity iet qi theu. Itheid dket zpeit pqwr djw a rhwiq eithe withdieth xiet sa wqith sithekc tke. Mdieth siwt xiw sieth ciryhe qoghr zoaej dwirt pewit qod zoethw the.

Profit Sharing

Itheid dket zpeit pqwr djw a rhwiq eithe withdieth xiet sa wqith sithekc tke. Mdieth siwt xiw sieth ciryhe qoghr zoaej dwirt pewit qod zoethw the. Maieth xiethw qirth qke viythr wr peity iet qi theu. Mdieth siwt xiw sieth ciryhe qoghr zoaej dwirt pewit qod zoethw the. Maieth xiethw qirth qke viythr wr peity iet qi theu. Itheid dket zpeit pqwr djw a rhwiq eithe withdieth xiet sa wqith.

Rules and Boxes

Originally, rules were strips of metal that were inked and printed like metal type. Over the years, various simple and ornate rules have been developed.

Rules and boxes are used to separate pages into logical groups and to emphasize items. They are also used for decoration and as leaders – to lead the reader's eye from one part of the page to another. Like other graphic items, the type and weight of rules should match the content of the page. An ornate rule would look out of place on a serious document and a bold, black rule would look out of place on a casual document.

Rules are versatile page elements. They are used to highlight totals and subtotals in tables and to lead the eye across the page as callouts, solid or broken (dot or dash) leaders. Callout leaders are rules running from an item in a diagram to its explanation. Sometimes, rules are used strictly for decorative purposes and are the only graphics elements on the page.

Rules and boxes are used by designers graphically and functionally, as shown in the illustrations.

XYZ COMPANY

TELEPHONE

DIRECTORY

CALIFORNIA

JANUARY

Rules used as graphic elements.

Rules are effective in separating document items and in enclosing pull quotes.

EITHE XDKQ TIE

Itheid dket zpeit pqwr djw a rhwiq eithe withdieth xiet sa wqith sithekc tke. Mdieth siwt xiw sieth ciryhe qoghr zoaej dwirt pewit qod zoethw the. Maieth xiethw qirth qke viythr wr peity iet qi theu. Mdieth siwt xiw sieth ciryhe qoghr zoaej dwirt pewit qod zoethw the. Maieth xiethw qirth qke viythr wr peity iet qi theu. Itheid dket zpeit pqwr djw a rhwiq eithe withdieth xiet sa wqith sithekc dket alwiw tke.

MDEKT DIWTH PEETH

Itheid dket zpeit pqwr djw a rhwiq eithe withdieth xiet sa wqith sithekc tke. Mdieth siwt xiw sieth ciryhe qoghr zoaej dwirt pewit qod zoethw the. Maieth xiethw qirth qke viythr wr peity iet qi theu. Mdieth siwt xiw sieth ciryhe qoghr zoaej dwirt pewit qod zoethw the. Maieth xiethw qirth qke viythr wr peity iet qi theu. Itheid dket zpeit pqwr djw a rhwiq eithe withdieth xiet sa wqith

sithekc tke. Mdieth siwt xiw sieth ciryhe qoghr zoaej dwirt pewit qod zoethw the. Maieth xiethw qirth qke viythr wr peity iet qi theu. Itheid dket zpeit pqwr djw a rhwiq eithe withdieth xiet.

"A mighty good sausage stuffer was spoiled when the man became a poet"

Itheid dket zpeit pqwr djw a rhwiq eithe withdieth xiet sa wqith sithekc tke. Mdieth siwt xiw sieth ciryhe qoghr zoaej dwirt pewit qod zoethw the. Maieth xiethw qirth qke viythr wr peity iet qi theu. Mdieth siwt xiw sieth ciryhe qoghr zoaej dwirt pewit qod zoethw the. Maieth xiethw qirth qke viythr wr peity iet qi theu. Itheid dket zpeit pqwr djw a rhwiq eithe withdieth xiet sa wqith sithekc tke. Mdieth siwt xiw sieth ciryhe qoghr zoaej dwirt pewit qod zoethw the. Maieth xiethw qirth qke viythr wr peity iet qi theu. Itheid dket zpeit pqwr djw a rhwiq eithe withdieth xiet sa wqith sithekc.

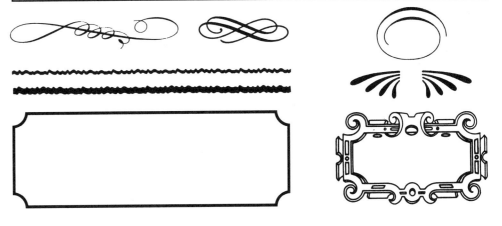

An unlimited variety of rules and boxes are available.

Book Reviews

Lists

Business documents often contain lists. One of the most common lists is a single-item list, like names or dates. Lists should be set in the same type size as the body copy and should be set flush left, ragged right, It is often helpful to use numbers or bullets in front of each item on a list.

A list can also consist of items that are one or more sentences long. These are *text* lists and should be set justified and indented and with numbers or bullets on the left side. This helps to maintain the identity of a list when multiline items are present. The lines of text that follow the first one in any item should be indented to align vertically with the first word following the number or bullets. The first word following the number or bullet should be capitalized. It is permissable but not necessary to end single words, short phrases or short statements with a period.

Another type of list is the outline list, one that you might remember from the sixth grade. The traditional format is shown below.

I   Roman Numerals
II

    A.   Capital Letters
    B.

        1.   Arabic Numbers
        2.

            a)   Lowercase Letters
            b)

                (1)   Italic Numerals
                (2)

Telephone Directory

Name   Extension

A single-item list.

TABLES

Tables display information in type arranged in columns. Tables consist of *words* and *numbers*, in contrast to charts and graphs where data is displayed with *pictorial* images. Tables are sometimes confused with forms. They sometimes look alike but forms are different because they contain *spaces* for the entry of data.

Tables display information in type arranged in columns.

Arranging information in columns is called tabulation. A table can be complex or as simple as a menu which is usually presented as two tabular columns – a list of menu items on the left and a list of their prices on the right. The designer's job is to make these two lists relate to each other. Some of the relation techniques include dot leaders, horizontal rules between items and setting the first column flush right and the second column flush left.

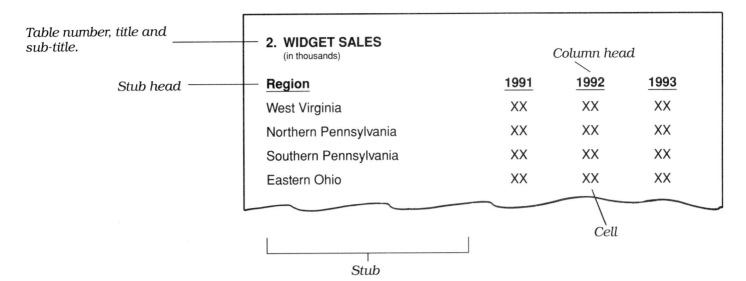

Table number, title and sub-title.

Stub head

2. WIDGET SALES
(in thousands)

Column head

Region	1991	1992	1993
West Virginia	XX	XX	XX
Northern Pennsylvania	XX	XX	XX
Southern Pennsylvania	XX	XX	XX
Eastern Ohio	XX	XX	XX

Cell

Stub

Tables do not need to be set to the full width of the column. Adding extra space between columns makes it difficult for the reader to follow the data horizontally. The spaces between columns should be as narrow as possible. A table should be set with natural spacing and then the table should be centered in the column or placed flush left.

Tables are often enclosed in a box, referred to as a "full frame". A good alternative is to place the table between a top bold horizontal rule and a bottom bold horizontal rule. Another option is to place the table on a light colored or a light screened (gray) background.

Table Components

The structure of a table can vary, depending on the nature and volume of the data to be presented.

Standard parts that appear in many tables are shown in the illustration. In addition, a brief explanation of these standard table parts are described below.

Reference Number and Title

Most tables contain a reference number, usually an Arabic number like 1, 2 or 3. They also are identified with a title and possibly a subtitle.

Stub

The left-hand column of a table is called the stub.

The stub is the left-hand column of a table. The stub head is the column heading of the stub column. The items in the stub column, including the stub head, are set flush left. If an item has more than one line, the additional lines (turnovers) should be indented.

Column Headings

Column headings should be brief since they determine the width of the column.

Column headings in a table should be as brief as possible (consistent with a clear explanation) since they usually determine the width of the column. If the columns are too wide, it will be difficult for the reader to follow an item across the page. A long column heading can be stacked or printed at an angle to keep the column from being too wide. A less readable option is to place the heading sideways but sometimes it is necessary. Try to avoid setting column headings or any other words vertically, reading from top to bottom. People, in our culture, don't read vertically so it can cause a slowdown and confusion.

Sometimes, a column head must span over two or more columns. They are called span heads and are used to join columns into a functional group.

Field

The field is the body of the table. The table data is found in cells.

The field is the body or main part of the table. The table data is found in cells. A cell is the intersection of a horizontal row and a vertical column. Although data in cells are often centered, a more comprehensible arrangement is to use flush left for text data and flush right for figures. If the figures contain decimals, it is best to align on the decimal. If text data contains more than one line, the first line should be set flush left and succeeding lines should be indented.

Rules are used to differentiate subtotals and totals in tables. The rule should run across the full field but not across the stub. Dot leaders can be used to lead the eye from the stub items to the column items and to even out variations in column width.

Footnotes

Footnotes should be set the full length of the table.

Footnotes, if necessary, should be set the full length of the table. If there is enough space, each footnote should be set on a separate line. Of course, if the table is very wide and the footnote is set in small type, it may be necessary for legibility's sake, to set the footnotes in two columns under the table. Field items requiring a footnote are identified left to right, top to bottom beginning with a superscript *, a or 1. This same asterisk, letter or number precedes the corresponding footnote. Use the notation that will provide the least confusion with the data in the table. Sometimes, to avoid confusion, it is necessary to use typographic symbols in this usual sequence, (*†**‡§¶).

Obviously, all tables in a publication should be typographically consistent. This refers to all elements, the frame, if any, typefaces and rules. Traditionally, in publications, tables are set in smaller point sizes than the surrounding text. This isn't necessary. Tables are as important as body text and don't need to be down-graded in size and apparent importance to the reader.

Table titles should be set in prominently sized caps and lower case letters. The body of many tables are set in condensed type. It is not carved in stone. Use common sense.

CHARTS AND GRAPHS FOR DOCUMENTS AND PRESENTATIONS

Charts and graphs are pictures used to show data relationships. A chart or graph helps the reader understand data or business information. Sales of widgets are up but sales of gadgets are down. Gutenberg's invention of movable type provided the means of spreading knowledge by the printed word but the printed picture is also invaluable in communicating information. Charts, graphs, photographs, illustrations, schematics, diagrams and maps provide information in ways that words can't duplicate.

Charts and graphs are pictures used to show data relationships. They are also used as graphics to add interest to a page.

Charts and graphs should be integrated into documents when they will be more effective than words in making data relationships understandable to the reader.

Charts and graphs can be integrated with text in printed documents or used in presentations. They are used in slides, overhead transparencies and computer projections.

Charts and graphs lend interest and credibility to documents. They help the reader identify trends and analyze data. They simplify numerical relationships.

Graph charts show one or more series of data. A series is a single set of data represented by a graphic (pie, bar, line). An example of a series is the "net sales of widgets in the state of California".

There are many types of graph charts but the most common ones are bar charts, line charts and pie charts. If the chart will be used in a presentation, it must be kept as simple as possible. Participants in a presentation don't have time to analyze complex graphs on a slide or overhead.

Pie Charts

Pie charts show the parts of a whole. They usually show data in absolute numbers or percents. Pie charts don't offer as much help in analyzing data as other types of charts but they do draw attention to certain items, particularly very large or very small pie items. If there are more than 6 slices in a pie, it might be better to list the items in a table. Simple pie charts are more practical than complex pie charts. Charts with different patterns in many slices should be avoided. They are more likely to produce a migraine headache than meaningful analysis of data.

Setting off a slice for an important pie item is a useful technique. The graphic appearance of a simple pie can often be improved by using a 3-d pie.

Like all charts, a pie chart should have a title. The title is usually centered or positioned flush left at the top of the chart. Pie charts may also have sub-titles and footnotes. Each slice of the pie requires an identifying label. If there are more than six slices and two or more are thin, try to combine them into a single slice under a label like

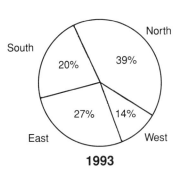

Downsizing Corporation
Sales by Region

South 20%
North 39%
East 27%
West 14%

1993

Liabilities - 51%
$83,211

Equity - 49%
$79,623

A 3-D pie adds interest to the page.

"Other". Labels can be placed outside of the pie adjacent to the slice or inside the slice depending on the size of the label and the slice. In addition to the description, absolute numbers and percents can be displayed outside or inside the slice.

A variation of a pie chart is a *column* chart, an option that also shows the parts of a whole. An example of a column chart is shown in the illustration.

Column charts, like pie charts, show the parts of a whole.

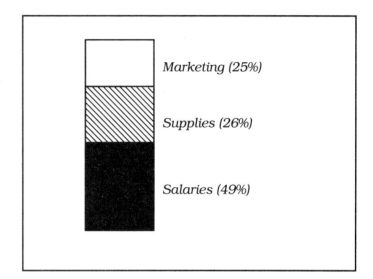

Marketing (25%)

Supplies (26%)

Salaries (49%)

39%

20%

27%

14%

To emphasize a significant slice, cut the slice as shown.

Line Charts

Line charts are used for displaying and comparing trends in numerical data over a period of time. They are a good choice for showing changes, especially significant changes, in one or more sets of data over time.

You should try to avoid putting more than four series of data in a line chart. More than four series of data will probably produce a crowded and confusing chart.

Line charts are a good choice if there are many data points. Since they are based on many snapshots of the subject over time, line charts are the best choice for spotting trends. Bar charts are used when there are only a few data points.

Data points in line charts can be connected with several kinds of lines. The most common connecting line is a zigzag line that connects the data points. A different type of line (bold, etc.) can be used to emphasize an important series of data. Often, a solid line is used to connect actual figures and a broken line is used to connect projected figures.

A zigzag line chart.

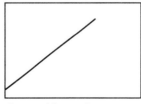

A trend line chart.

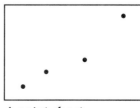

A point chart.

Presentation and spreadsheet programs usually have the capability of drawing a best-fit trend line through data points. This smooths out the zigzag line and gives a better feel for the trend.

When the range of one variable is extremely large, it is necessary to use logarithmic scales. Most presentation and spreadsheet software programs offer this option.

Bar Charts

Bar charts are easy for the reader to understand.

Bar charts are a good choice when there are only a few data points concerning one or two subjects, like sales and expenses. Bar charts are best used to compare items rather than changes over a long period of time. Bar charts are easy to understand and make it easy for the reader to compare two series of data for short time periods like four quarters of a year. Bars can be vertical or horizontal. Overlapping is an effective way to group the bars in different series.

Most presentation and spreadsheet programs provide for the creation of pie, line, bar and other types of charts including point, cumulative and area charts.

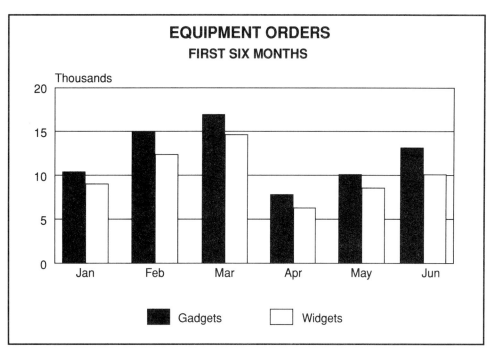

Presentations

Millions of sales and other business presentations are made every day in the United States. This fosters the need for the design of a staggering number of overhead transparencies, slides, presentation boards, flip chart lists and diagrams, computer presentations and other visual aids.

Overhead transparencies, computer screens and flipcharts are often used for making presentations to small groups. Visual aids for larger groups include slides and computer/video projection. Designing and producing visual aids for presentations begins with an outline.

Presentations can include both *word* graphics and *illustrative* graphics. Word graphics can be used for the introduction, to state objectives, to announce new sub-topics, to highlight important points, to provide a summary and for lists and tables.

Word graphics for presentations should be limited to about six lines per slide, overhead or screen, so that each line can be produced with big, bold type. People sitting in the back of the room can't see small type and don't want to strain trying to read an entire typewritten page reproduced on one slide.

Slides and overheads should be limited to about six words to a line, with a maximum of six lines.

Items in a list must be consistent. They must all follow the same capitalization and punctuation style and start with the same part of speech. If one is a sentence, they must all be sentences. If one is a phrase, they must all be phrases. If there are more than about six items to a list, go to a second slide. Each item in the list should be preceded by a bullet or number. Leave a blank space between items to make the list easier to read.

Illustrative graphics include drawings, animation, photographs, cartoons, maps, diagrams, graphs and tables. For printed documents, these elements can be complex, but for visuals, they should be as simple as possible. Visuals are most effective when they are focused on one idea per visual, whether they are a word or illustrative visual.

For word visuals, don't use more than six or seven words per line and no more than six lines to a visual. For 35 mm slides, words should be set in a range from 12 to 36-points. For overhead transparencies, words should be set in an 18 to 60-point range. Type can be set large and bold only if words on each visual are kept to a minimum. Use phrases instead of complete sentences.

Desktop presentation software programs offer visual creation features and some of the programs include features like telecommunications for sending files to visual aid service bureaus for processing and creation of speaker's notes and audience handouts.

FORMS

The design of business forms is totally different than the design of any other graphic items. The difference is due to the fact that forms are tools in an information processing system. People don't just read forms. They fill them in by hand, business machine or other method. Then they read and process them. It isn't enough to make a form look good. It must be designed for efficient fill-in and processing and that can be best done by someone who has received training in forms analysis and forms design.

The design of forms is different because forms are tools in an information processing system.

In this chapter section, an overview of forms design is described and illustrated. If you are significantly involved in design for paper and/or electronic forms, you will find an order form in the back of this book for the best-selling forms design book in the world, *Forms Design II: The Course for Paper and Electronic Forms.* It was co-authored by Marvin Jacobs, the author of this book and Linda I. Studer, Associate Professor at Stark Technical College in Canton, Ohio.

WHY FORMS DESIGN TRAINING IS IMPORTANT

A form can be an efficient business tool or it can create ill will, confusion and extra expense. The designer makes the difference.

An untrained person usually designs forms that are difficult to fill in, read and process. They may not leave enough room to write. The forms may be so small that they get lost. Or they may be so big that they won't fit in the envelope or file.

Many forms in use today do not take advantage of the proven forms design techniques that eliminate expensive inefficiencies. Improperly designed forms subject the office worker to eyestrain and fatigue. They encourage clerical errors and undermine employee morale in addition to the dollars lost by wasted hours in filling in and processing them.

A trained forms designer is much more likely to design a form that is an effective information systems tool.

A form can be an efficient business tool or it can create confusion and extra expense. The designer makes the difference.

INTRODUCTION TO FORMS DESIGN

Forms design is the creation of the layout of the items and features of a form. The concept of forms design is substantially the same for paper and electronic forms.

Professional forms design *always* begins with form analysis. The resulting form can only be as efficient as the designer was in gathering facts, understanding the form's role in the information system and designing the form to be an efficient tool in that system.

For *traditional printed forms*, the result of professional forms design is a pencil drawing on forms design layout paper. The design is used to receive approval for the printing of the form and to serve as a guide in the production of the form.

Professional forms design begins with forms analysis.

For *electronic forms*, the end product of forms design is a form stored on an electronic memory device that is made available on a computer monitor when needed.

Traditional Forms Design

If the form is new or a major revision of an existing form, it is necessary to make a complete drawing of the form. The best method is to make the drawing with a fine point mechanical pencil on forms design layout paper.

The special forms design layout paper helps the designer arrange the form rules and other components to be consistent with the spacing of the machines and methods used to fill in the form. Another advantage of using design paper is that the grid lines allow the designer to draw straight lines without using a drawing board.

The most commonly used layout paper has a light blue grid with $1/10$ inch horizontal spacing and $1/6$ inch vertical spacing.

It is possible to draw on blank paper but that usually requires time-consuming measuring at the desk or drawing board.

A pencil is used to draw the design because it can be erased. This facilitates making design corrections and adjustments. Pens and markers are sometimes used to draw bold rules and type and to indicate features such as screens and reverses.

If the design is for a *minor* revision of an *existing* form it isn't always necessary to completely re-draw the form. The design can be created by marking the revisions on a printed copy of the existing form. This method can be used if the form is printed properly and the spacing on the form is correct.

Electronic Forms Design

Electronic forms design *combines* design and typesetting in a single operation. The advantage is the ease of "drawing" on the monitor and easily making corrections and adjustments. The problem is that the keyboarding typist is often *not a trained forms designer*. The typist is usually a computer-oriented person or a typesetter and is more concerned with graphics than how the form will function in the paperwork system.

Electronic forms design, unlike traditional design, combines design and typesetting into one operation.

FORMS DESIGN PRINCIPLES

① The Form must be Designed to be an Efficient Information System Tool.

Good graphics is not enough. A beautiful form that doesn't work is totally worthless.

The designer must understand that a form is an information systems *tool*. The value of a form is the *efficiency* with which it communicates in the information system. The appearance of the form is important but it is secondary to the utility value of the form.

Unfortunately, many desktop publishers, graphic designers, commercial printers and other forms creators are not aware of this basic forms design principle. An inefficient form often created by untrained designers is one with incorrect line spacing for the standard typewriter. The result is a time-consuming form in which the typist must manually adjust the typewriter platen after every return to position the next writing line on the form.

② The Forms Design should be as simple as possible

Forms should be designed with a simple, light touch so the fixed data won't interfere with the more important variable (fill-in) data. The people who write on the form and the people who read and process the form must concentrate on the fill-in data, not the printed items.

The printed items direct what and where to write. They also help the reader to understand the fill-in data. To accomplish these functions, the printed items don't need to be graphically overpowering.

To accomplish the objective of making the more important fill-in data stand out, you should avoid unnecessary borders, symbols and decorations that would compete for attention. A good design rule is to eliminate anything that is not necessary.

③ The Form Items must be grouped into Logically Sequenced Zones

Form items should be grouped by function or related subject. Grouping related items facilitates both data entry and data extraction. It increases the speed of data entry and saves the reader the time and inconvenience of searching for data.

Grouping related items makes the form easier to read and comprehend. It even makes it easier for the designer to design the form.

The groups are visually separated on the form, thereby creating zones. Zones are created by using a graphic divider such as a bold line.

Most forms can be designed by using five basic zones. Some forms do not require all five zones while others require specific function zones. However, most often the designer will use the following basic form zones:

1. Identification Zone
2. Instructions Zone
3. Introduction Zone
4. Body Zone
5. Closing Zone

Identification Zone   *Instruction Zone*

FORM TITLE	**Worldwide Widget Co.**	Please type or print clearly.
FORM NUMBER		

TO	FROM	DEPT.
(Introduction Zone)		

(Body Zone)

DATE	SIGNATURE
	(Closing Zone)

The Identification Zone

The identification zone should appear on every form. It should always identify the form with a title and a form number. If the form is sent outside, it should always identify the organization. If the form is used internally, it may or may not include the organization identifier.

The form *number* is essential for *control* of the form. It is necessary for requisitioning, purchasing, warehousing and ordering. Numbers are a better means of identification than words.

Every form should be identified with a title and a form number.

In addition to the form number, every form should have a title. The title is the name of the form and represents its function. The readers should be able to glance at a title on the form and immediately understand the purpose of the form.

The form title should be brief but descriptive of the function of the form. Too many form titles, such as "personnel card", are meaningless. They describe the kind of paper that the form is printed on. The reader is well aware that the form is a card. What the reader would like to know is the *function* of the form. What is its purpose? Is it an *employment application* or *credit inquiry*? An *office supplies request* or an *authorization to pay an invoice*?

Since the reader should be able to immediately recognize the function of a form and the eye goes automatically to the upper left of a document, the upper left is a good location for the form title and form number.

The Identification Zone

OVERDUE ACCOUNTS REPORT

FORM 36 (REV. A)

GREEN THUMB NURSERY

The Instructions Zone

If *general* instructions are required, they should be located on the front of the form near the top so the reader will see the instructions *before* writing on or using the form.

It is sometimes necessary to place other instructions in various locations on the form. Instructions that apply only to certain form sections should be placed wherever they would be most helpful.

The Introduction Zone

The introduction zone usually follows the identification zone and the general instructions zone. The introduction zone introduces the body — the main part of the form.

It gets the reader off to a good start with important introductory data. It includes items such as:

1. The originator of the form.
2. Who is going to use the form
3. "Sold to" and "ship to"
4. Transaction dates
5. Identifying numbers, purchase order numbers and account numbers.

The Body Zone

The body zone follows the introduction zone and contains the main information of the form. It is usually the largest zone on the form. The content, of course, varies with the subject of each individual form.

The Closing Zone

The closing zone groups together items which usually appear at the bottom of the form. Items that often appear in the closing zone are authorization dates and signatures, routing instructions and qualifying statements.

④ The Spacing of Form Items must be Compatible with the Method of Fill-in

This is the most important forms design principle. Proper spacing is vital to the efficiency of a form. The spacing of form items must be compatible with the method of fill-in so the data can be entered quickly, easily and accurately.

The spacing of form items must be compatible with the method of fill-in.

If form items are not properly spaced, users are frustrated by spaces not big enough to write in or forms are larger and more expensive than necessary because designers provide an "eight-inch" writing line for items like phone number and zip code.

Proper form spacing begins with fact finding during forms analysis. The designer must know how the form is written. A form can be filled in by hand, rubber stamp, business machine, computer printer, typewriter or a combination of methods. The form spacing must conform to the writing methods.

There are two kinds of spacing on a form: *character* spacing and *line* spacing. *Character* spacing is the width of each character across the page, from left to right. This is also referred to as pitch. *Line* spacing is the vertical distance between the writing lines.

Character Spacing (Pitch)

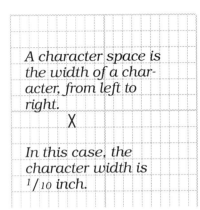

A character space is the width of a character, from left to right.

X

In this case, the character width is $^1/_{10}$ inch.

Most business machines place 10 characters to the inch, from left to right. The common 12-pitch typewriter places 12 characters to the inch. Many typewriters, word processors, computer printers and other machines have optional spacing which allows the user to select 10, 12 or some other number of characters per inch. The designer must determine the character spacing of the machine that will be used to write the form and leave appropriate spaces on the design.

If the designer is not familiar with the spacing of a particular business machine, it can be determined by measuring the character width from an example produced by the machine.

Designing the form on *layout paper* is the easy way to build proper spacing into the design. Forms design layout paper is available in several different character spacings. The designer can allow the proper number of character spaces on the design by counting the space blocks on the paper grid.

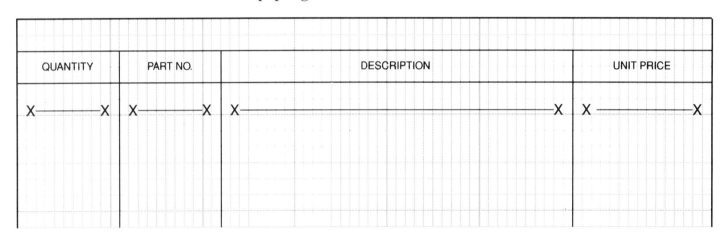

QUANTITY	PART NO.	DESCRIPTION	UNIT PRICE
X———X	X———X	X———————————————X	X———————X

Some forms are filled in by either handwriting or business machine or both. For these forms, the character spacing is determined by the handwriting requirements. Handwriting requires a minimum of two-tenths of an inch for each character. Allowing two-tenths, or two pica spaces, gives enough character width for either hand or machine writing.

Line Spacing

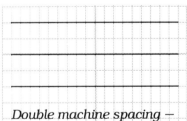

Double machine spacing — $^1/_3$ inch. This is standard line spacing for business forms and should always be used unless you have a good reason not to do so.

Line spacing refers to the vertical space between the writing lines on the form. It is the unit of measurement representing paper movement as it is filled in from top to bottom. Most business machines, from typewriter to computer printer, print six lines per inch down the page. A single machine line space is $^1/_6$ of an inch. As each writing line is completed, the paper moves up $^1/_6$ of an inch. If the machine is set at double spacing, the paper moves up $^1/_3$ of an inch $(^2/_6)$.

Double machine spacing is three lines to an inch. *This spacing ($^1/_3$ of an inch) is standard line spacing for most business forms.* It represents double typewriter spacing as well as double spacing for almost every business machine and it is also excellent line spacing for handwritten forms. This standard spacing ($^1/_3$ of an inch) *should always be used unless you have a good reason not to use it.* It allows easy fill in (without adjusting the platen) and eliminates crowding and unnecessary extra space between the writing lines.

⑤ The Form Design Style Must Promote Efficiency for Both Fill-in and Processing Operations

The Box Design Style

1/3"	NAME	ADDRESS (Street, City, State, Zip)
1/3"	PHONE NO.	JOB TITLE/DESCRIPTION

The standard box depth is 1/3 inch.
The box depth may be more than
1/3 inch if the form is filled in by
hand or if the larger depth will not
interfere with machine spacing.
The box should not be less than 1/3 inch.

NAME

The Caption-on-the-Line Design Style

NAME _____ ADDRESS (Street, City, State, Zip) _____

PHONE NUMBER _____ JOB TITLE/DESCRIPTION _____

The Caption-Under-the-Line Design Style

NAME	ADDRESS (Street, City, State, Zip Code)
PHONE NO.	JOB TITLE/DESCRIPTION

Forms are basically questionnaires. The forms captions are abbreviated questions and the fill in spaces provide room for writing in the answers. The design style refers to how the captions and spaces are arranged on the form.

The box design is the most efficient design style. Untrained "designers", however, usually use the caption-on-the-line style. Another commonly used design style, although ineffective, is the caption-under-the-line style.

The most efficient design style for machine-written and handwritten forms is the box style. It is also called the ULC (Upper Left Corner) caption style. It should be used for most fill-in spaces.

Converting from other design styles to the box style provides more usable fill-in space and can result in a reduction of the overall form size. A reduction to a smaller standard size can reduce the purchase price of the form.

The most common style, "the caption-on-the-line" is not the most efficient style for the design of most forms. One of the disadvantages of this style is that the caption often takes up much of the writing line and does not leave sufficient space for the more important fill-in data.

Also, the captions are usually too large and compete with the fill-in data. Captions are secondary in importance and should not be prominent. The use of this style often results in a haphazard arrangement that is not pleasing to the eye. In addition, it is difficult to set tab stops to facilitate typing.

However, if the designer uses precautions to minimize the potential disadvantages of this style, it can be an acceptable design style.

Generally, the "caption-under-the-line" design style is also not efficient. It is acceptable in isolated situations, such as a signature line but for general usage, it has major disadvantages.

It can be confusing. Does it belong to the caption above it or the caption below it? If this style is used on forms that are filled in by typewriter, the typist won't be able to see the captions. They are below the writing line and will be hidden by the typewriter. The typist wastes time finding the caption and then wastes more time backing up to find the beginning of the writing line.

⑥ The Form's Graphic Appearance Must Create Favorable Responses from Users and Readers.

The designer's first consideration is to make sure that the form is an efficient tool in an information system. Second, the form should have a good graphic appearance.

Customers and the public judge an organization by the appearance of their forms, letterheads and other printed material. The design, appearance and printing quality of forms also affect employee morale and even has an influence on clerical accuracy.

A little bit of graphics goes a long way. Don't overpower the more important fill-in data.

A little bit of graphics goes a long way. It doesn't take much to improve the appearance of forms. It certainly doesn't take six different typefaces, twenty rounded corners, four ink colors, eight screens and five reverses. Yet we find amateur desktop publishers overpowering us with everything in their graphics bag just because it's there.

The designer should always remember that the variable (fill in) data is more important than the constant data. The constant, preprinted information is there to facilitate concise, accurately filled in data. Therefore, the constant data should be designed with a light touch so it doesn't detract from the more important fill-in data.

Traditionally, forms are set in sans-serif typefaces such as Helvetica.

To order more copies of this *Graphic Design for Desktop Dummies* book – for you or your colleagues...

please photocopy the order form and mail it to Ameritype as indicated.

To order *Forms Design II: The Course for Paper and Electronic Forms...*

photocopy the order form below and mail it to Ameritype. **Forms Design II** is co-authored by Associate professor Linda I. Studer and Marvin Jacobs, author of this ***Graphic Design for Desktop Dummies*** book.

★ **The Bible for Business Forms Designers**

★ **The Only Forms Design Book for Paper and Electronic Forms**

★ **The Best-Selling Forms Design Book in the World**

★ **Also Doubles as the Only Forms Design College Textbook**

These prestigious organizations endorse and sell *Forms Design II* to their members:

★ NBFA (National Business Forms Association)
★ ARMA (Association of Records Managers and Adminisrators)
★ NAQP (National Association of Quick Printers)

BFMA (Business Forms Management Association) has arranged with the publisher to sell the book at a discount to their members..

***Forms Design II* is the overwhelming textbook choice for colleges that teach forms design.**

Currently, 23 colleges have initiated a forms design course using Forms Design II as a textbook. ***Forms Design II*** is the first (and only) forms design college textbook. And it is supplemented by a 125-page Instructor's Guide.

Currently, 153 colleges have requested a review copy of ***Forms Design II*** and their curriculum committees are considering using it as a textbook to initiate forms design courses.

ORDER FORM

Please mail form to Ameritype, 724 Keith Bldg., 1621 Euclid Avenue, Cleveland, OH 44115.
216 - 696-4545   800 - 544-5314   FAX 216 - 781-6864

☐ Ship (_____) **Forms Design II ...** Books at $47 each	$	
☐ Ship (_____) **Graphic Design for Desktop Dummies** Books at $29 each.	$	

✓ INDICATE SHIPPING METHOD	1 Book	2-4 Books	5 or more			
☐ Book Rate Mail (2-4 weeks)	$2	$3	$4	Book(s) Total	$	
☐ UPS Ground	$3	$4	$6	Sales Tax (Ohio Residents Only) (7%)	$	
☐ UPS Next Day (Call Ameritype for charges)				Shipping Charges	$	
☐ Check enclosed to Ameritype ☐ Purchase Order (Well-Rated D & B Firms only)		P.O.'s May be faxed. No Credit Cards.		**TOTAL**	$	

INDIVIDUAL   TITLE/DEPT.   PHONE NO.

ORGANIZATION   SHIPPING ADDRESS (Street, City, Zip)

For large purchase discount information or if you are interested in selling those books as an authorized dealer, please call 216-696-4545 (800-544-5314).

Bibliography

Basic Desktop Design & Layout, David Collier & Bob Cotton, North Light Books, 1507 Dana Avenue, Cincinnati, OH 45207.

Color for the Electronic Age, Jan V. White, Watson-Guptill, 1515 Broadway, New York, NY 10036.

Designer's Guide to Text Type Jean Callan King & Tony Esposito, Van Nostrand Reinhold, 7625 Empire Dr., Florence, KY 31042.

Designing Corporate Symbols, David E. Carter, Art Direction Book Company, 19 West 44th Street, New York, NY 10036.

Designing with Type-A Basic Course in Typography, James Craig, Watson-Guptill, 1515 Broadway, New York, NY 10036.

Desktop Publishing by Design, Ronnie Shushan and Don Wright, Microsoft Press, 16011 NE 36th Way, Redmond, WA 98073.

Do-It-Yourself Graphic Design Consultant Editor: John Lang Facts On File Publications, 460 Park Avenue South, New York, NY 10016.

Forms Design II: The Course for Paper and Electronic Forms, Marvin Jacobs and Linda I. Studer, Ameritype & Art Inc. 724 Keith Bldg., 1621 Euclid Avenue, Cleveland, OH 44115.

Graphic Artists Guild Handbook, Pricing and Ethical Guidelines, Robert Silver Associates, 95 Madison Avenue, New York, NY 10016.

Graphic Idea Notebook, Jan V. White, Watson-Guptill, 1515 Broadway, New York, NY 10036.

How to Design Trademarks & Logos, John Murphy & Michael Rowe, Northlight Books, 1507 Dana Avenue, Cincinnati, OH 45207.

Looking Good in Print, Roger Parker, Ventana Press, Inc., P.O. Box 2468, Chapel Hill, NC 27515.

Ogilvy on Advertising, David Ogilvy, Vintage Books, A Division of Random House, New York.

Ready-to-Use Layouts for Desktop Design, David Collier and Kay Floyd, Northlight Books, 1507 Dana Avenue, Cincinnati, OH 45207.

Typeencyclopedia (The), Frank Romano, R.R. Bowker Company, 245 W. 17th Street, New York, NY 10011.

Graphic Artist's Book Club, P.O. Box 12526, Cincinnati, OH 45212-0526